MORE
URBAN
LESS
POOR

Sida    from Routledge

First published by Earthscan in the UK and USA in 2006

Copyright © Sida and the authors, 2006

ISBN-10:   1-84407-381-5   paperback
ISBN-13:   978-1-84407-381-8   paperback
ISBN-10:   1-84407-382-3   hardback
ISBN-13:   978-1-84407382-5   hardback

Cover design, book design and layout by Eva Vaihinen, Press Art

For a full list of publications please contact:
Earthscan
2 Park Square, Milton Park, Abingdon, Oxon, OX14 4RN
711 Third Avenue, New York, NY 10017

Earthscan is an imprint of the Taylor & Francis Group, an informa business

A catalogue record for this book is available from the British Library

Library of Congress Cataloging-in-Publication Data

Tannerfeldt, Göran.
    More urban, less poor : an introduction to urban development and management /
Göran Tannerfeldt, Per Ljung.
        p. cm.
    ISBN-13: 978-1-84407-381-8 (pbk.)
    ISBN-10: 1-84407-381-5 (pbk.)
    ISBN-13: 978-1-84407-382-5
    ISBN-10: 1-84407-382-3
        1. City planning–Developing countries. 2. Urbanization–Developing countries.
        3. Urban poor–Developing countries. I. Ljung, Per. II. Title.
    HT169.5.T36 2006
    307.1'216091724–dc22

                                                                        2006010023

MORE
URBAN
LESS
POOR

**an introduction to urban
development and management**

Göran Tannerfeldt & Per Ljung

Foreword

The world we are living in – and the world we continue to build together – is the product of many forces, including globalization and urbanization. But urban scenarios are surprisingly neglected, and often misunderstood, in the larger development context. Rural and urban life and economies are often seen as quite separate, but they are more intimately linked and inter-dependent than many realise.

Our rapid conversion to an urban society presents large challenges everywhere, even if the symptoms take many different forms in different countries. Many view urbanization as negative and threatening, since it is easy to point to growing slum areas, environmental degradation and social gaps. But cities contribute to development, and urbanization is both a requirement for – and a result of – economic, cultural and social develop-ment. The aim is to promote sustainable cities where all citizens have opportunities to improve their living conditions.

Göran Tannerfeldt and Per Ljung describe how urban problems can be solved. They place city planning, infrastructural issues, housing, etc in the larger context of governmental controls, financial issues and social goals. And they expose many gaps. But they also provide many examples of how to break the patterns of urban poverty.

A prerequisite for this type of change is economic growth, which cities generate and which can be strengthened by infrastructure improvements and institutional reforms. But a well-considered pro-poor policy is also required, which the authors explain in some detail.

More Urban – Less Poor provides a holistic view that will appeal to politicians and civil servants with responsibility for urban development. But it also provides guidance to coming generations, from all sectors of society, working with city planning, social sciences and cultural geography – as well as those engaged in development cooperation at any level.

This book has been financed by the Swedish International Develop-ment Cooperation Agency (Sida), which supports comprehensive urban programmes in developing countries and in countries with transition eco-nomies. It is Sida's hope that it will make a timely contribution to those who are enthusiastically working towards sustainable urban development – the creators of urban life.

Thomas Melin
Head of the Division for Urban Development
Department for Infrastructure and Economic Cooperation
Swedish International Development Cooperation Agency (Sida)

CONTENTS

CONTENTS

TABLES

Note: Tables are also to be found in the Annexes

BOXES

Urban café life in Hanoi, Vietnam.

© Jean-Léo Dugast / PHOENIX

Acknowledgements

The authors are very grateful to everyone who contributed to this book.

First and foremost we would like to thank David Satterthwaite at the International Institute for Environment and Development (IIED) and Ann Elwan of PM Global Infrastructure. Both of them contributed substantively to this book and took the time to read and comment on the drafts, making invaluable contributions in the process.

We are also very grateful to other reviewers who read the drafts and provided advice and relevant comments: Gordon McGranahan, IIED, Diana Mitlin, IIED and University of Manchester, Alfredo Stein, HDM Lund University, Pelle Persson, Cities Alliance, Kristina Boman, Boman & Peck, Michael Söderbäck, OECD/DAC and Gabriel Marin, SIPU. Many others – including Sida staff in Stockholm and abroad – have provided useful information and observations, improving the book in many ways.

Gordon Evans worked hard to make the prose flow and read well and Robbin Battison provided indispensable copyediting.

Finally we would like to gratefully acknowledge that this book could never have been written and produced if Sida had not financed it as a tool for its work in urban development.

Summary and conclusions

Nearly all future population growth will be in the cities and towns of the developing world. These are growing at an unprecedented rate; soon the rural population will be less than the urban, while the number of urban dwellers living in poverty is increasing.

Contrary to general belief, the main contributor to urban growth is not rural-urban migration, but the natural population increase. However, migration to the city is the key factor behind the change in proportion between urban and rural population, which we call urbanization.

Urbanization is a historic shift. The agrarian economy and rural culture, which over thousands of years changed only very slowly, is, in just a couple of generations, being replaced. Emerging is a dynamic society with a diversified economy based on industrialized production, specialised services, communication and even international trade. The cultural, social and political consequences of this transformation are enormous and the long-term effects difficult to foresee and therefore difficult to plan for. Urbanization is inherent in economic and cultural development and the trends are universal. Local conditions may temporarily speed up or slow down the process but urbanization can neither be stopped nor reversed.

The first chapter of this book is about urbanization in developing countries. The scale and nature of urban poverty is discussed in the following chapter, and chapter three explores the major challenges for sustainable and equitable development. Ways to meet the challenges and manage rapid urban growth are then outlined in chapter four, and the final chapter proposes how development cooperation should contribute.

Urbanization and economic development

The transition from a predominantly rural to a predominantly urban society is a complex process with many contradictory and controversial aspects. The transition provides opportunities and benefits, but also has negative consequences: poverty and inequality; slums and environmental degradation; social instability and lack of security. These problems, however, are not inherent to urbanization – and they can be managed. In a period of rapid change, the challenge may seem overwhelming, but there is a dynamic. Given the strength of an urban economy and with good governance, over time, the problems we see today will be overcome.

Urbanization is a consequence of, but also a requirement for, economic development. An increase of income per capita has, in every country, been

accompanied by urbanization. Often two-thirds of GDP is generated in major cities housing perhaps one third of the total population. However, deficient infrastructure and poor urban management limits urban productivity, which could contribute even more to national economic development and poverty reduction

The importance of the informal economy is still widely underestimated. A majority of the urban population – and especially the poor – actually earn their wages or run micro-businesses in the informal economy. Instead of being promoted as a healthy initiative, this vital sector of the economy is often hampered by misguided policies and obsolete regulations.

This book is about urban development, but urban and rural development are complementary. In fact urban development promotes rural development and vice-versa: a growing urban economy creates a growing market for agricultural products, which prompts agriculture to develop; urban centres can absorb the rural underemployed, thus improving rural productivity, and the compound effect is raised income per capita in rural areas. The diversification of the economy to include and develop other sectors besides agriculture should be promoted, if the poorest countries are not to continue to produce only low value goods and thus remain poor. The development of the agrarian economy cannot be achieved without a growing urban economy, but an increase of rural incomes also promotes urban development.

Poverty and slums

The most salient negative aspect of urban growth in developing countries is the conditions of the urban poor. Their number is underestimated and

A majority of the urban population earn a living in the informal economy.

© Magnus Rosshagen

growing. At least 40 per cent are poor, and with present trends, in 2020 there will be more than 1.4 billion slum dwellers. The UN Millennium Development Goals (MDGs) call for "significant improvement in the lives of at least 100 million slum dwellers" by 2020. For such a target to be meaningful, it is recognized that the formation of new slums must also be prevented. Affordable land and services for housing another 600 million people are needed. Achieving the targets would halve the number of slum dwellers by 2020.

Towns and cities in developing countries are unable to provide housing, infrastructure and services in pace with their population growth, which is typically much faster than it ever was in Europe. The result is unplanned shantytowns without basic services, where conditions are miserable. This encourages politicians and donor agencies to regard urbanization as negative. But growth of slums is neither an inevitable consequence of urbanization, nor can it be blamed only on the lack of financial resources. Slums are also the products of failed policies, bad governance, inappropriate legal and regulatory frameworks, dysfunctional markets, unresponsive financial systems, corruption, and not least, a lack of political will. Some governments even compound the problems by limiting access to land and services for low-income migrants. But policies to stop migration or compelling people to leave urban areas – even through massive evictions – are futile. This hounding of the poor has instead made their life even harder.

The multi-faceted problems of the growing urban centres in developing countries will require action on both national and local levels. The private sector and civil society, including community organizations, have to be involved. Broad and sustainable urban development depends on political leadership committed to a democratic and equitable vision of urban society, together with transparent and capable urban management systems. Policies, governance and legal frameworks must be reformed; this is fundamental.

Without explicit pro-poor polices there will be no improvement for the urban poor. The point of departure must be to recognize the realities of the poor, their assessment of the situation and their priorities. Urban poverty is different from rural poverty and a better understanding of its nature is required from governments and donors. Health indicators in slum areas are at least as bad as in rural areas, but other aspects of urban poverty are even more specific. Pro-poor urban policies need, for example, to address the fundamental lack of safety and security and provide protection against forced evictions, crime, corruption, violence and the numerous other risks confronting the urban poor. Harassment of the informal sector should stop; affordable land, housing options and basic services must be made available. Education and health services must reach also those living in informal settlements. HIV/AIDS is particularly serious in urban areas and present efforts to counteract the pandemic are insufficient.

Governance and urban management

Local governments should have a key role in all aspects of urban development, but in most developing countries they are still very weak. Strengthening democratic self-governance at the local level is critical. The slow decentralising of responsibility and authority to this level needs to be accelerated and supported by fiscal reforms and other means to increase the financial resources. The devolution of power to local authorities, however, must be accompanied by governance reforms and a strengthening of their institutional capacity.

Urban development planning needs to involve all stakeholders and be comprehensive and holistic. Cities Alliance through its 'City Development Strategies' has provided a promising model for a participatory process aiming at a collective vision and an action plan for economic growth, environmental improvement and poverty reduction at the local level.

One of the most critical issues for the poor is the lack of affordable land and basic services for housing. More effective land and housing markets should be promoted through regulatory reforms, but local authorities also have to face the land issue in a pro-active manner. Legalisation of informal settlements, provision of tenure security and improved basic services are urgent measures.

The environmental situation of urban centres in developing countries is unsustainable. Most serious are the health-threatening sanitary conditions of the slums. Air and water pollution, poor management of hazardous waste and the depletion of natural resources are other examples. Information and education creating better awareness are part of the solution. Service provision can be enhanced in several ways. Solutions are available. Not all are costly, but major investments are required as well.

Culture is an important dimension of sustainable development. Media and communication, educational opportunities and human interaction and innovation are features of urban centres and are vital for the development of the country as a whole. The lack of access to culture and the lack of recognition of the culture and of the cultural heritage belonging to the poor are further dimensions of poverty.

Ultimately, all development must build on domestic resources and the efforts of the people themselves. Success depends on the enabling of these efforts and the mobilising of human and financial resources. New approaches are needed to finance municipal services, infrastructure and housing. Attracting domestic private capital is a key issue. Utility reforms, financial accountability and stable revenue flows are then required. The micro-finance sector in general and housing micro-finance in particular should be promoted, and the concept of saving for a family home needs to be encouraged.

The role of development cooperation

A goal for development cooperation is to contribute to an environment supportive of poor people's own efforts to improve their quality of life. With respect to urban development it should be pursued through contributions that:

- make it possible for the urban poor in slums and squatter areas to improve their living conditions,
- strengthen democratic governance and the empowerment of local authorities,
- facilitate the urban contributions to economic growth,
- reduce the environmental burden caused by urban activities,
- promote cultural development including cultural heritage management.

The vision proposed here is:

that towns and cities in the developing countries shall become equitable and sustainable urban societies – veritable engines of economic, social and cultural development that will benefit urban as well as rural populations.

Development requires the involvement of all parties including the private sector and civil society. Particularly important is that the poor are not treated as passive recipients, but recognized as active participants. Human rights and gender equality are key issues. In all cases the consequences of the HIV/AIDS pandemic have to be taken into account.

Urban development is a local matter but highly dependent on central level policies, national institutions and resource allocation from central government. Both central and local levels thus need to be addressed in development cooperation. Preference should be given to projects that create an enabling environment and build capacity or produce replicable models. But this is not enough. The badly needed upgrading and expansion of obsolete urban infrastructure in the least developed countries cannot take place without large-scale financial support and harmonized efforts from the donor community are required.

The first generation of Poverty Reduction Strategy Papers (PRSPs) failed to develop definitions and indicators that would allow an adequate assessment of urban poverty. As a consequence, these strategies did not address the issue appropriately. It is important that governments and donors ensure that the particular characteristics of urban poverty are better understood and taken into account when poverty reduction strategies are prepared or revised, or when impact is monitored.

Similarly, it is important that sector-wide cooperation programmes in health, education, water, environment, etc take proper account of the needs of the urban poor. This would require a specific analysis based on the understanding that the conditions for people living in urban slums differ from that of people in more prosperous parts of the city, but also from the conditions of the rural poor.

Finally

Neither governments nor donors are meeting the challenges of rapid urban growth. The result is crisis: more poverty, more slums, more environmental degradation. This crisis can be confronted: urgent, wise and concerted action could ensure a sustainable urban development. Understanding the issues – our purpose here – is imperative, and the first step towards a more humane urban world – more urban indeed, but less poor.

1. AN URBANIZING WORLD

The rapid growth of urban centres in the developing world is unprecedented. Urbanization and economic development go together. Urban and rural development are linked.

The majority of the world's population will soon live in urban areas – this is true for developing countries as well as for the developed world. Most of the world's population growth will take place in the urban areas of poor countries.

Urban growth continues

Most people will soon live in urban areas

Urbanization is not a new phenomenon. Babylon (600–400 BC) had an estimated population of 350 000, Rome (150 BC–350 AD) reached 1.1 million inhabitants and the population of Angkor (900–1100 AD) in present Cambodia was 1.5 million (Schneider, 1960).

World-wide urbanization, however, belongs to the 20th and 21st century. While the developed world was already highly urbanized by the 1960s, most developing countries were just starting the process.

FIGURE 1.
The urban population in developing countries will soon surpass the rural population according to UN statistics and projections.

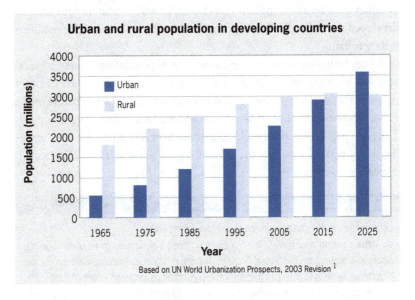

Urban and rural population in developing countries

Based on UN World Urbanization Prospects, 2003 Revision [1]

By about 1900, Great Britain was the first country with more people living in urban than in rural areas. Parts of Latin America followed and have been more urbanized than many European countries since the first half of the 20th century. Over 90 per cent of the population of Argentina and Uruguay for instance, now live in urban areas compared to 83 per cent in a country like Sweden. At the other end of the scale some Sub-Saharan countries have a low urbanization level.

1) Data are revised bi-annually and published the following year (see p 164).

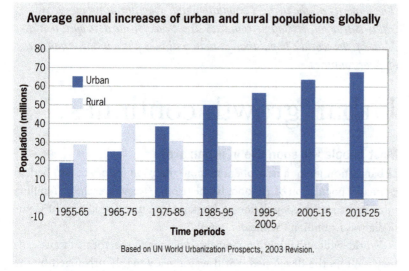

Average annual increases of urban and rural populations globally

Population (millions)

Urban
Rural

80
70
60
50
40
30
20
10
0
-10

1955-65 1965-75 1975-85 1985-95 1995-2005 2005-15 2015-25

Time periods

Based on UN World Urbanization Prospects, 2003 Revision.

FIGURE 2.
The population increase almost entirely takes place in urban areas. Soon the rural population will start to decrease according to UN projections.

According to UN data more than half of the world's population will live in urban areas by 2007, and ten years later this will also be true for the less developed countries. Even in Africa, many countries will soon be predominately urban.

Since the beginning of the 1970s the rate of population growth in rural areas has been falling. In the more developed regions and in parts of Latin America the rural population started to decrease in absolute numbers in the 1950s. Some 65 years later this will also happen in less developed countries. The rural population in several African countries is likely to continue growing slowly beyond 2030, but the devastating impact of AIDS could lead to a decrease even there.

Box 1: Urbanization and urban growth

Urbanization and urban growth are two distinct concepts.

Urbanization here means the transition process from a rural to an urban society, where the proportion of the total population living in urban centres increases while the proportion living in rural areas decreases.* This urbanization is an effect of rural-urban migration, but is also due to other demographic factors. These are discussed below under 'Understanding urbanization', where the economic and social reasons behind the process are described.

Urban growth here means the growth of the urban population and not the geographical expansion of urban centres – although this normally is a consequence. In-migration is one reason for urban growth, but natural population increase is a more important factor.

Most cities in developing countries experience high rates of both natural population growth and migration. The combined effect is very rapid urban growth.

* See Annexes, Definitions.

Future growth of the world's population will almost entirely take place in the urban areas as shown in Figure 2, and it is mainly in the cities and towns of the less developed regions where these people will live.

Unprecedented urban growth in developing countries

Now, in the beginning of the 21st century, the average yearly urban growth rate in the least developed countries is 4.3 per cent, but some of these countries experience rates of 6 per cent and above. Individual urban centres in developing countries could have much higher rates. Some large cities saw compound annual growth of 7–10 per cent for the second half of the 1900s (Annexes, Table A10, p 177).

FIGURE 3.
Same urbanization pattern but different time lag. The graph shows the urbanization level between 1960 and 2002 for developing countries at three income levels. In 2002 the low-income countries had the same urbanization level as lower middle income countries 30 years earlier. In 2002, the lower middle income countries were as urbanized as upper middle income countries were in 1960.

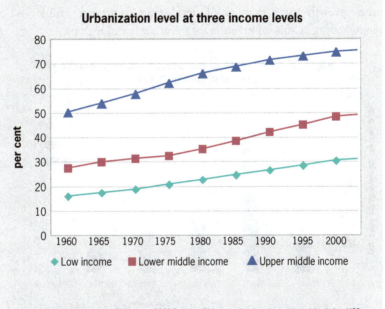

Based on UN World Urbanization Prospects, 2003 Revision GNI per capita: Low-income countries below USD 735 (eg Bangladesh, Ethiopia, Nicaragua, Tanzania, Tajikistan); lower middle income countries USD 736-2935 (eg Bolivia, Guatemala, Kazakhstan, Romania, Serbia and Montenegro, South Africa); upper middle income countries above USD 2935 (eg Botswana, Costa Rica, Croatia, Mexico)

The increase of the urban population in the developing world is striking (Tables A1, p 165 and A6, p 172). Between 1985 and 2003 the urban population of these countries increased from 1.2 to 2.1 billion and is expected to reach 3.2 billion in 15 years time. Migration rates do not differ much from Europe, but the higher rate of natural population increase makes urban growth in the developing countries unprecedented. (The growth rate of a city like Berlin, for example, never exceeded 4 per cent even during its peak.) Urbanization is a fundamental transformation of society, with far-reaching economic, social, cultural and political consequences. To manage rapid urban growth is a major challenge – especially for poor countries with a weak institutional framework.

In view of the magnitude and implications of this ongoing change it is surprising that the international donor community has only given it limited attention.

Regional differentials

Behind global figures there are important differences between regions and countries and also within countries and cities.

Tables A4-6 (Annexes pp 168–173) show the urbanization level and the urban growth for a number of developing countries. Tables A1-3 (pp 165–167) give this information for major areas and regions.

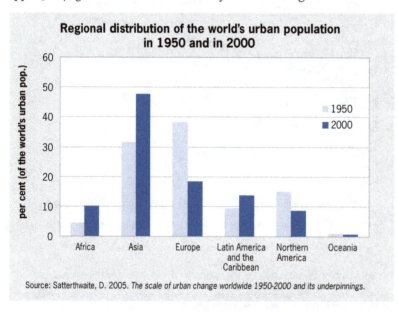

Regional distribution of the world's urban population in 1950 and in 2000

per cent (of the world's urban pop.)

Source: Satterthwaite, D. 2005. *The scale of urban change worldwide 1950-2000 and its underpinnings.*

FIGURE 4.
Regional distribution of the world's urban population in 1950 and in 2000. Europe and North America taken together now account for less than 30 per cent of the world's urban population, a decline from well over 50 per cent in 1950. Soon half of the world's urban residents will be in Asia.

Latin America is most urbanized

Latin America is the most urbanized of the four regions. More than three-quarters of the people live in urban areas. In South America the Figure is 81 per cent and in Central America 69 per cent. The urban growth rate in Latin America as a whole has slowed down and is under 2 per cent today. However, in poor countries like Nicaragua, Honduras and Bolivia the urban growth rate is higher – especially for the bigger cities.

Since the 1980s the entire population increase of the region has occurred in urban areas, and the rural population has decreased.

Rio de Janeiro, with 12 million people, is one of the world's largest cities. Like most megacities its annual rate of population growth has slowed down and is expected to average only 0.9 per cent throughout 2000-2015.

© Pietro Cenini / PHOENIX

Asia – soon one and a half billion urban people

Asia, with more than 1.4 billion people living in cities and towns, has almost 50 per cent of the world's urban population. The urbanization level is close to 40 per cent and the average annual urban growth is 2.5 per cent. In many countries the rural population has already started to decrease, and by 2015 this will be true for Asia as a whole – a remarkable shift. Part of the region has enjoyed strong economic growth and reduced poverty, but Asia also has the largest slum population in the world – more than half a billion.[3] Air and water pollution are serious and the environment is deteriorating in most urban areas.

Some countries in Asia are still predominantly rural – Laos, Cambodia and Bangladesh, for example – but these countries have high annual rates of urban growth: 4.6, 5.5 and 3.5 per cent respectively.

Shantytown in Mumbai, India.

© Thomas Melin

Urbanization is fastest in Africa.

As for Asia, the level of urbanization in Africa is almost 40 per cent, but with a much smaller urban population (0.3 billion). Sub-Saharan Africa – except for Southern Africa – is the region with the fastest growing urban population. Several countries have an annual urban growth rate of more than 5 per cent, but census data are often old so statistics and projections are uncertain. In the past, UN projections based on old data tended to overestimate future urban growth. In parts of Africa the HIV/AIDS epidemic is likely to slow down the process of urbanization and urban population growth.

In Africa there are large variations. At one extreme we find Southern Africa with an urbanization level of 54 per cent and at the other, Eastern Africa with only 26 per cent.

Uganda, Ethiopia, Eritrea, Malawi, Rwanda and Burundi are among the poorest countries in Africa and still have more than 80 per cent of their population in rural areas. However, these countries also have very high rates of urban growth; a growth which is expected to continue for at least another three decades.

A bar in Kibera slum area, Nairobi.

© Magnus Rosshagen

Poverty, inequality and depopulation in European transition countries

Countries like Albania, Bosnia-Herzegovina, Moldova and Serbia-Montenegro have only 45–52 per cent of the population living in urban centres while Russia, Belarus and Macedonia are predominantly urban. Urban population growth is low in most countries of the region and some of the transition countries even have negative urban growth because of increased mortality and declining fertility.

Belgrade, Serbia.

© John-Olof Vinterhav

---

3) Poverty in terms of material resources. See also 'The nature of urban poverty' p24

Urban poverty in the European transition countries has grown dramatically since the early 1990s. The urban poor are twice as numerous as the rural poor. Recent estimates reveal that 10 per cent of the urban population live in slum-like conditions in very crowded housing. Privatization of the huge rental housing stocks has lead to segregation and urban inequalities have increased. The HIV/AIDS pandemic spreading at catastrophic rates adds to the seriousness of the social situation. The issues are further discussed in 'Urban challenges in the transition countries' (p 77).

Box 2. Are data and projections reliable?

The main references for statistics on demographic change and urban growth are the United Nations *Demographic Yearbook* and *World Urbanization Prospects*. Censuses and surveys, such as the Demographic and Health Surveys (DHS), are the primary data sources. In addition, there are numerous case studies. It is generally agreed that the statistical information on urbanization and urban growth is insufficient and much of it is of dubious quality. The UN statistics are based on data provided by governments and definitions of 'urban' vary. An urban centre in one country may be classified as rural in another. Administrative divisions may define the outskirts of a city as a rural area in spite of huge informal settlements located there – and so on. The different national definitions affect mainly the smaller settlements, which might be classified as either rural or urban. As a consequence, the absolute numbers of urban populations can be questioned, but are likely to be underestimates, since many small towns and some peri-urban areas are not included.

The UN projections are based on extrapolating past trends into the future. In the absence of recent census data, for many poor countries they have been based on previous projections rather than actual data. For this reason the projections have failed to reflect changing trends and, so, for example, overestimated urban growth in Africa during a period of economic decline when migration rates fell. The UN projections are 'mechanical' and do not take into account economic change and other factors affecting urban growth in a particular country or city.

In spite of these statistical deficiencies, it is still possible to compare data over a period of years, both between and within countries. Better statistics and more refined projections would be welcome, but would not add much to the general picture of rapid urban growth and progressing urbanization in the developing countries.

It should be noted, however, that global urban statistics are influenced by a few big countries, especially China and India, but also Brazil, Indonesia, Nigeria, Pakistan and Iran.

Gender-specific data are generally not available and aggregate statistics do not show the enormous intra-urban differentials in terms of income, service provision, living conditions etc. In many countries informal settlements are not recognised and may not be taken into account in the statistics.

The urbanization process is inherent in economic and cultural develop-ment and the trends are universal – local factors can temporarily speed up or slow down the process but it can neither be stopped nor reversed.

Understanding urbanization

Urbanization is a historic shift. The agrarian economy and culture, which only changed slowly over thousands of years, is – over a few generations – being replaced by a dynamic society with a diversified economy based on industrialized production, specialised services, communication and interna-tional trade. The cultural, social and political consequences of this transfor-mation are important and the long-term effects difficult to foresee.

Why do cities grow?

Natural increase contributes more than migration to the growing populations in urban centres, but rural-urban migration is an important factor in less urbanized countries. Migrants often come from other, smaller, urban centres.

Sixty per cent of urban population growth in developing countries is natural growth. Around 30 per cent is the net effect of migration and 10 per cent is explained by changed boundaries and other administrative measures, which obviously have an effect on the statistics.[4] One must, however, always keep in mind that these figures are estimated and aggregated and that there is great variation among regions and countries. Migration contributes more to urban growth in the early stages of urbanization. This is the case now for many Sub-Saharan countries.

Urban centres typically have a population with a high proportion of people of reproductive age. Birth rates tend to be high and mortality rates low. This explains why natural population growth is high even though urban dwellers tend to have fewer children than their rural counterparts.

Migration is an economic phenomenon in the sense that the prime driv-ing force is the search for a better income. Other factors may contribute but are secondary. Civil wars, ethnic conflicts, natural disasters and other external factors have often reinforced this process. People forced to leave their villages to seek protection tend to stay on in the cities if they cannot safely return within a relatively short time.

In several countries a major reason for migration is the lack of arable

The 'glocal' economy: Telephone traders wait for customers at the computer village mar-ket in Lagos, Nigeria. Peddlers of pirate soft-ware now hold sway on the same streets where drug dealers and prostitutes swarmed a decade ago. Every building is packed with computer and mobile phone companies.

© Scanpix-AP/George Osodi

4) Montgomery, Mark R, Stren, Richard, Cohen, Barney and Reed, Holly E (2004) *Cities Transformed: Demographic Change and its Implications in the Developing World*, For the Panel on Population Dynamics, National Research Council, Earthscan, London

land or lack of access to such land. Because of population growth more and more ecologically sensitive land is being cultivated, but there are limits to how large a population it can support. Migration may be the only solution. In other countries, for example in Latin America, the problem is the land-ownership structure rather than any real shortage of land.

Traditionally, migration has been seen as an individual one-way move from a rural village to a city, but the reality is far more complex. It is rather a matter of population mobility. Only one-third of migrants actually come from rural areas.[5] The rest have lived in other cities or in small urban centres. Thus, the migrants to large cities are not primarily rural-urban migrants. The implications of a considerable inter-urban circulation may be quite different from the implications of rural-urban migration.

International migration is an important and growing phenomenon in many countries. For instance, it is estimated that 10 per cent of Guatemala's population has migrated to the USA.

Migrants are usually fairly well informed in advance through relatives, friends and others about the conditions they may expect. Case studies in Kenya, India, Philippines and Thailand show that many migrants have jobs waiting for them when they arrive, usually in the informal sector. A study in Khartoum found that urban employers often recruit new workers by asking current employees to recommend family members or friends. Information chains and social networks seem to be as important for internal migration as they are for international migration. Migrants also often do better economically than is generally believed.

Rural-urban migrants are young and often better educated. Education, information and communications seem to promote rural-urban migration. Increased migration can be observed during periods of economic growth and when there are great urban/rural differentials in terms of economic conditions or economic opportunities.

Studies confirm that migrants make rational choices. For a great number of individuals urban life is perceived as 'good' or at least 'less bad' – in spite of all difficulties. A decision to migrate is like an investment decision. There are economic risks and social costs. Returns are greatest for the young, for whom the increased income can be discounted over a longer period, and for the better educated, who have greater employment opportunities.

Migration could be regarded as the dynamic response to changing economic realities and is, in itself, a positive contribution to economic development in urban as well as rural areas. Barriers to urbanization and migration could be barriers to economic development.

---

5) Findings based on DHS. Source see footnote 4.

Urbanization and economic development go together

There is no economic development without urbanization. Attempts to curb urbanization may have an adverse effect on economic development. Large cities are most productive.

Economic development and urbanization are closely linked. Countries with higher GDP and income per capita usually are more urbanized. This is shown in Figure 5. One possible explanation of this positive relationship is that urbanization facilitates economic growth. An equally plausible explanation is that economic development stimulates urbanization. In other words – urbanization could be seen as a *consequence* of but also as a *requirement* for economic development.

From the beginning of civilisation, cities have been administrative and cultural centres, places for sophisticated manufacturing and services, and nodes in extensive trading networks. The economic functions of towns and cities everywhere and through history are more similar than we usually think. These similarities indicate that urbanization is a phenomenon inherent in economic development.

Indeed, urbanization is driven by some well-established economic relationships. In a certain sense, the driving force is 'Engel's Law', which postulates that, as income increases, the share of the income devoted to food

FIGURE 5
Urbanization and economic development go together.
Some highly urbanized countries appear to have a low income level, which may be explained by a temporary economic recession – economic success is more easily reversed than is urbanization.
It is important to note that countries measure 'urbanization level' in different ways.

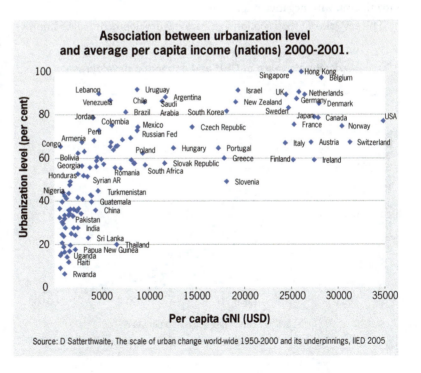

consumption declines (ie the portion of income spent on non-agricultural goods and services grows). Thus, the share of agriculture in GDP declines drastically as a country's economic development increases (Fig 6).

The urban economy in low-income countries as well as in high-income countries is related to economies of scale and agglomeration that make enterprises in large cities more productive than those located in small towns or rural areas. Agglomeration economy is founded on a large number of factors, such as: a large and diversified pool of labour (which in turn improves labour productivity); a greater local market, making it easier to reap the benefits of scale in production; easier access to suppliers and specialised services; lower information and transaction costs; and, because of easier face-to-face meetings and more diversified contact networks, an environment that encourages innovation. The results of agglomeration economies are clearly shown in Table 1. Urban centres account for a much larger share of GDP than the population share. Thus they are in fact 'engines of development'.

In Africa, it seemed towards the end of the 20th century as if there was 'urbanization without economic growth'. Revised statistical data, however, suggest that the population increase in urban centres slowed down during this period, as in other regions during periods of economic decline. (As explained earlier, urban populations may increase due to natural population growth even with negative migration.)

The key role of urban economy in national development makes improv-

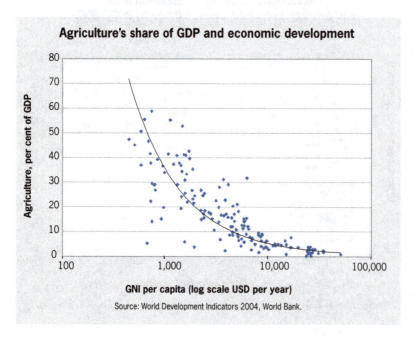

Agriculture's share of GDP and economic development

Agriculture, per cent of GDP (vertical axis: 0, 10, 20, 30, 40, 50, 60, 70, 80)

GNI per capita (log scale USD per year) (horizontal axis: 100, 1,000, 10,000, 100,000)

Source: World Development Indicators 2004, World Bank.

FIGURE 6.
The share of agriculture in GDP decreases with economic development. The vertical scale shows agriculture as a percentage of GDP and the horizontal shows GNI per capita (log scale USD per year). The dots represent developing countries from all regions.

Country	City	Share of Population	Share of GDP (per cent)	Relative Productivity (per cent)
Table 1. Urban productivity. Larger cities are more productive.				
Mexico	Mexico City	14.2%	33.6	465
	Other Urban Areas	45.9%	46.1	197
	Rural Areas	39.9%	20.3	100
Kenya	Nairobi	5.2%	20.1	489
	Other Urban Areas	6.7%	10.2	192
	Rural Areas	88.1%	69.7	100
India	All Urban Areas	19.9%	38.9	256
Turkey	All Urban Areas	47.1%	70.1	263

Relative productivity is GDP per capita in the urban centres compared with GDP per capita in rural areas, which has been set to 100 per cent.

Based on Freire, Mila and Mario Polèse, *Connecting Cities with Macro-economic Concerns: The Missing Link*, World Bank 2003.

ing urban productivity a strategic task. Constraints hampering urban productivity are: deficient infrastructure, inappropriate regulatory frameworks, weak municipal institutions, corruption and inadequate financial services, as well as environmental degradation, health and unsanitary conditions, violence and crime.

Megacities

Very large cities are not typical. Less than 4 per cent of the population in developing countries live in cities with more than ten million people.

Most people think of urbanization in terms of fast growing 'megacities' such as Mexico City, Calcutta or Lagos. Their size and growth is fascinating and threatening. Many 'prophets' in the 1970s predicted their collapse, because such huge agglomerations had never existed earlier, and they seemed to challenge all previous experience of societal organization. But the prophets may have been wrong and the growth of those very large cities continues, although at a slower pace.

The annexed Tables A8-10 (pp 176-177) provide data on the size and growth rate of the world's largest cities. There were 22 urban agglomerations with more than 10 million inhabitants in 2003. The growth of large cities in absolute numbers is impressive. Between 1950 and 2000 Mumbai, Delhi, Dhaka and Jakarta each grew by about 200 000 people per year. The average population increase of both Sao Paulo and Mexico City was 300 000 per year, and Tokyo grew by 464 000 per year during the same period.

Still, many of the largest cities have not grown as much as previously anticipated. Mexico City, for example, had 18 million people in 2000 and not 31 million people as predicted 25 years earlier. Calcutta, Sao Paulo, Rio de Janeiro, Seoul, Chennai (former Madras) and Cairo are other cities with several million inhabitants less than projected. Mexico City, Calcutta and Sao Paulo had more people moving out than in during the 1990s, but still experienced large increments of their population because of natural increase.

However interesting, megacities are not typical, and it is unfortunate that they often dominate the discussion on urbanization in developing countries. Less than 4 per cent of the total population and 9 per cent of the urban population in developing countries live in cities of more than 10 million people (2003). The majority of those cities are located in just three nations: China, India and Brazil. In more than 50 countries the largest city has less than half a million inhabitants. It is also worth noting that five of the fifteen largest cities in the world are in developed countries (Japan, USA, Russia).

While the megacities are an interesting phenomenon, they need to be analysed case by case. Here the intention is to deal with the more typical features of urbanization and urban growth in developing countries.

Can urban growth be controlled?

Many governments (and donor agencies) tend to regard urbanization as negative and have tried various means to stop or reduce rural-urban migration.

Governments in most developing countries are not capable of managing rapid urban growth. As a result, more and more people live in unplanned, often illegal shanty-towns, with limited access to basic services and with environmental conditions that threaten life and health. The political response has often been attempts to stop migration and even to force people to move out again. Such policies – including forced evictions – have failed. Only totalitarian governments in China, South Africa under apartheid, Cambodia during Pol Pot's regime and recently Zimbabwe have temporarily managed to halt urban growth through repressive means. In China, however, the policy is changing and urbanization is now being seen as promoting economic growth.

Realising that it is impossible to stop urban growth by force, many governments – with donor support – have implemented programmes to encourage potential migrants to stay in rural areas. Success has been limited and the effects even counter-productive, since rural development pro-

It is called **Murambatsvina** ('Restore the order'). In fact it is the ruthless eviction of informal settlements and the destruction of the informal economy in Harare, and other cities in Zimbabwe. It started in May 2005 and continued during June and August. Twenty-five settlements were bulldozed, 700 000 of the poor lost their homes and an estimated total of 2,4 million people were affected. This action is a sad example how the group in power – for political reasons – chooses to treat a large share of the population as unwanted people with no rights. It is also a showpiece of how the leadership lacks understanding of the importance of the informal economy and concern for the living conditions of the urban poor.

Residents of Kambuzuma township with their belongings, including a portrait of Zimbabwean President Robert Mugabe, foreground, look on as a bulldozer demolishes their homes in Harare, Zimbabwe Friday, June 3, 2005. Zimbabwean police are under orders to destroy 'illegal dwellings' and vendors' shacks as part of a campaign to clean up the city. (AP Photo)

Source: www.omvarldsbilder.se
050818

grammes bringing better education, information and communication seem to promote rather than prevent migration. Such programmes, as well as the promotion of alternative production in rural areas, are not an alternative to continued urbanization, but can improve living conditions for the rural population locally.

Deshingkar and Anderson have made a relevant observation:

> Although not stated explicitly, many rural development programmes aim to strengthen *in situ* development and so stem mobility. The underlying rationale can be found in the literature on common property resource management and agricultural development that is replete with statements of expected declines

in migration flows due to successful employment creation and resource regeneration... Current trends in population mobility and urbanization suggest that policy needs to become more flexible to provide services to people who are on the move. New arrangements that can provide migrant workers with access to critical information on labour markets and rights as well as basic services in health, education, shelter and food are needed.[6]

Generally, policies have wrongly been based on the assumption that urban growth could be confined if migration was reduced. However, since net migration, as we have seen, only accounts for about 30 per cent of urban population growth, 85 per cent of the growth would remain even if migration was halved (which in reality is impossible).

In some countries, policy makers may have hoped that by not providing land or services for low-income groups, migrants would be discouraged from coming, and there would be less pressure. Such policies have made life even more difficult for the urban poor, but have not had a major impact on urbanization.

Another strategy to relieve pressure on the bigger cities and at the same time improve services for the rural population is to promote the development of small and medium-sized towns. This could support agricultural development (see below), but would not reduce migration.

To conclude, urbanization is a universal and irreversible process. It will continue whether we like it or not. External factors and internal policies may temporarily speed up or slow down the pace of urbanization, but in the long run they will not make much difference.

---

6) Deshingkar, Priya and Anderson, Edward (2004) *People on the move: New policy challenges for increasingly mobile populations*, ODI Natural Resource Perspectives no 92, Overseas Development Institute, London

Urban and rural development are complementary and are part of the same development process. The economic and social linkages are strong and make a sharp distinction between urban and rural misleading.

Urban-rural linkages

Household linkages

The connection between urban and rural life is very strong especially in newly urbanized countries. Rural-urban migration – as well as international migration – is often a strategy of 'income diversification' at an individual or household level. Cash earned in town is transferred to family members in the village, and farm products are brought to town and consumed or sold there. This is not accurately reflected in official statistics but case studies suggest that remittances represent a substantive contribution to rural households. Urban dwellers may go back to the village to help with the harvest and they often still own land farmed by relatives.

The ties weaken with time; later generations born in town do not maintain the same close ties. This is true for most Latin American countries, where large populations have lived in urban areas for generations.

Rural life is partly preserved by migrants to urban areas. Settlements on the outskirts of large cities and small or medium-sized towns may look very similar to rural villages. The absence of infrastructure, the same type of housing, and small-scale agriculture with pigs, chickens and goats are typical for these settlements. In parts of Asia, agriculture, cottage industries and housing coexist in areas within a 100 km radius of the city centre. Urban agriculture is discussed further in 'Earning a living' (p 48).

Economic linkages

A growing city with a growing economy is a growing market. The value of agricultural production often increases rapidly near these urban centres. This, together with the capacity of urban centres to absorb underemployed rural people, will raise the per capita income in rural areas (more income for fewer people). In the long run it is difficult to see how economic development, including productive and sustainable agriculture, can take place if the urban economy does not develop. Thus there is no contradiction between urban and rural development. It is worth noting that many of the highly urbanized countries are at the same time major agricultural producers (Denmark, Netherlands, Canada, Israel etc).

Secondary cities are important service centres for their rural hinterlands.

They link rural producers and consumers with the national and global markets. They are also important destinations for rural migrants. These towns prosper when agriculture develops, since agricultural growth generates more employment in local services and other non-farm activities than in agriculture. Unfortunately, they are often neglected by national governments. A strategy to strengthen these towns could support agricultural growth. It will not reduce rural-urban migration but may have an effect on intra-urban movements and relieve some pressure on the capital city.

National policies at macro-economic level in most developing countries previously had a strong urban bias. The effects of import-substituting industrialization policies and state controlled agricultural marketing boards of the 1960s and 1970s together with the growth of public sector employment and food subsidies contributed to favour sections of the urban population.

Middle and upper income groups in the capital city were particularly favoured. The structural adjustment programmes (SAPs), budget cuts and the liberalisation of economies have changed this pattern, and put an end to this urban bias. An 'urban favour' is of course that the economic and political power remains highly concentrated to the capital city.

The economic integration at national and global levels is a major trend influencing rural-urban economic relationships today. Even remote areas in poor countries are now becoming part of the global economy. The small local producers increasingly have to compete with products from large firms in the capital or with imported goods, and the return on local agriculture depends on world market prices. Urban services are indispensable if agricultural producers in developing countries are to compete in the global trade.

FURTHER READING

Montgomery, Mark R, Stren, Richard, Cohen, Barney and Reed, Holly E (2004)*Cities Transformed: Demographic Change and its Implications in the Developing World*, For the Panel on Population Dynamics, National Research Council, Earthscan, London

Cohen, B (2003) 'Urban Growth in Developing Countries: A Review of CurrentTrends and a Caution Regarding Existing Forecasts, *World Development, Elsevier*, vol 32 no 1, pages 23-51, January

2. URBAN POVERTY

Living conditions for the poor are very different in urban and rural areas. Urban poverty is underestimated and growing. In the least developed countries, 70 per cent of the urban population live in slums. Most people earn their income in the informal economy.

Crime and violence and a general lack of safety are major concerns for the urban poor. They depend on cash income for survival and the cost of living is high compared to rural households. Health indicators are often as bad as or worse than in rural areas.

The nature of urban poverty

What is urban poverty?

Poverty deprives people of the freedom to decide over and shape their own lives. Absence of economic margins and limited opportunities means that poor people are vulnerable.

Poverty is manifested in different ways: hunger, ill health, ignorance, discrimination and exclusion, denial of dignity etc. It is thus *multidimensional*. It is also *context-specific*. The particular features of poverty in any one place depend on the particular environment – socio-cultural, economic and political. Poverty is *relative* since it is defined by the poor in relation to what they judge to be a decent life. An important aspect is that poverty is *dynamic*. Its manifestations will change over time and people may move in and out of poverty.[7]

The situation of the urban poor, especially in larger cities, is different from that of the rural poor. It is important to understand the particular features of urban poverty. The first and perhaps most significant feature is that the urban poor depend on a cash income for survival. Most food – as well as cooking fuel and water – have to be bought. Building materials, even for the simplest shack, are expensive. Many of the urban poor live on the outskirts of cities. To earn money they often have to travel long distances and transportation is a major expense.

Some of the poorest people in Latin America and Asia, but also in African cities, live as tenants in blocks of flats in deplorable condition. Others are lodgers, common even in the poorest housing. These might not appear in official records; they are 'the invisible victims of urban poverty', since their needs are unnoticed and so not addressed in policy documents and development programmes.

Mass housing in the transition countries has been privatized (p 77). Tenants then become owners, but often without the resources to maintain those buildings; a gentrification process then leads to the formation of slums.

Social inequality is a salient feature of urban society.

---

7) From Sida (2002) *Perspectives on Poverty*, Stockholm.

Table 2. Infant and under five mortality rates and diarrhoea prevalence

Informal settlements in Nairobi (population 1.4 million) show worse conditions than rural areas. In Kibera, the largest settlement, with more than half a million inhabitants, almost one child in five dies before the age of five. (Mortality rates per 1000 births.)

Location	Infant mortality rate	Under five mortality rate	Prevalence of diarrhoea with blood in children under 3 in two weeks prior to interview
Kenya (rural and urban)	74	112	3.0 %
Rural Kenya	76	113	3.1 %
Urban Kenya excl. Nairobi	57	84	1.7 %
Nairobi (whole population)	39	62	3.4 %
Informal settlements in Nairobi	91	151	11.3 %
Kibera settlement	106	187	9.8 %
Embakasi settlement	164	254	9.1 %

Source: APHRC (2002), *Population and Health Dynamics in Nairobi's Informal Settlements*, African Population and Health Research Centre, Nairobi.

Even in a small district town in Tanzania, the richest household had an income 109 times greater than that of the poorest.[8] Poverty in relative terms is directly experienced by the urban poor. An understanding of urban poverty is impossible if the intra-urban social differentials are not taken into account.

Statistics on health, education and income, as well as average figures on access to and provision of schools, health facilities, water and sanitation seem to indicate that urban populations are favoured compared to people living in rural areas. But average figures are misleading. Child mortality in poor urban areas is much higher than in more wealthy areas. Case studies show that poorer groups in larger cities suffer comparable or even higher levels of disease and death than their rural counterparts. This is in spite of the fact that such cities have the best hospitals and no shortage of drugs. Table 2 shows how health indicators may vary for different settlements, even within the same city. The reason is that densely populated slums without access to safe drinking water or safe excreta disposal systems are a breeding ground for disease.

Illegal settlements often are not recognized by the authorities and, as a consequence, are deprived of public services. People living there are sometimes not represented in the statistics. An unplanned settlement such as Mathare Valley in central Nairobi, which has existed for forty years, and with a population of perhaps 200,000, is still not recognized, and therefore lacks adequate public health service and education.

---

8) Baker, J and Mwaiselage, A (1993) *Three Town Study in Tanzania*, Sida, Stockholm

Prodel is a Sida-supported urban poverty reduction programme in Nicaragua, which started in 1994, and now is run by a self-sustained institution, the Prodel Foundation.

During the first ten years Prodel initiated and co-financed more than four hundred participatory infrastructure projects in poor urban communities and provided ten thousand small loans for home improvements and twenty-four thousand loans to micro-enterprises. Including the third phase, which ends in 2008, close to 75 000 families will have benefited from 511 infrastructure projects. The total number of home improvement loans will amount to 29 000 and the number of micro-credits will reach 41 000 to 15 000 micro-enterprises.

The infrastructure works are implemented by the municipalities with a high degree of participation from the people concerned. About 60 per cent of the cost for each project is covered by the municipality and the community – the rest is a grant financed by Sida.

The loans are managed by several micro-finance institutions with credits from Prodel Foundation. A majority of the loans have been issued to women.

The loans are not subsidized and the conditions are set in order to make the revolving fund grow and the institution financially sustainable. By the end of 2003 the funds managed by the Foundation were over USD 5 million and are expected to reach 10 million in 2006 thanks to continued support from Sida and the financial income.

Prodel has managed to address several aspects of urban poverty in large number of poor neighbourhoods. The effects are increased income and local development, better housing conditions and infrastructure, improved municipal governance and empowerment of the poor.

In developing countries most of the rural poor can grow their own food, fuel-wood is available, and they can build their own homes using local materials. Little or no cash is needed. This does not mean that life is easy. Water and fuel-wood might be far away, the water not clean, and harvests are always uncertain. School and health facilities may also be a long walk away, and the quality often poor. Rural conditions are not equal either – and in most countries there are wealthy as well as poor and neglected regions.

The life of the poor is hard in rural as well as urban areas, but the problems are different, and need to be addressed accordingly. It is important that the particular features of urban poverty are taken into account in strategies for poverty reduction (PRSPs).

The urban poor are never safe

The urban poor live dangerously. The risks they face are different from those in a rural setting. The health risks have been mentioned and are further discussed in those sections dealing with environment, housing, water and sanitation. The prevalence of HIV/AIDS is higher, which means the risk of infection is greater (see 3.3.6p **). Crime, violence, fire, traffic accidents, earthquakes, flooding, and landslides are other risks, which are either typically urban, or have particularly devastating effects for the urban poor. Fires have razed entire settlements – for example, Marconi Beach in Cape Town, South Africa in 1996. The urban poor are also disproportionately victims of drug abuse and alcoholism. Many poor women – perhaps abandoned by the fathers of their children – are forced into prostitution. Children may end up as 'street children'.

In several countries criminal youth gangs – sometimes demobilised child soldiers from armed conflicts – are a veritable threat to the society. In urban areas social disintegration, crime and violence are a growing problem. The poor are more exposed than others. They cannot protect themselves, and the police are often corrupt and anyway hardly ever enter shantytowns.

Safety is an important aspect of urban poverty, and is a priority concern for the poor themselves. Field studies of urban poverty in the 1990s demonstrated that escalating levels of violence together with lack of access to clean water were the most important concerns of the poor. Several victimisation surveys confirm that the urban poor are the main victims of crime (but report crime the least). The poor have identified safety and security as a major concern in several studies; as important as hunger, unemployment and lack of safe drinking water. Unfortunately the issue has received little attention from national governments and donors.

Many risks are common to everybody, but men, women and children are exposed to particular dangers. Crime and violence affect men and women differently and the problem has to be seen from a gender perspective. Injuries and the occupational health hazards of the informal and small-scale industry affect men in particular. Women are victims of robbery and rape and suffer together with their children from burns and domestic accidents, smoke from open fires, and sanitary health hazards. The children, the disabled and the aged among the urban poor are particularly vulnerable.

The poor suffer most from natural disasters like earthquakes, hurricanes, flooding, and heavy rain. 'Naturally triggered disaster' would be a more accurate term. The natural event becomes a disaster when it hits vulnerable people. Building on unsuitable sites – low-lying land in a river delta, or on steep slopes with no storm water drainage and no retaining walls are disasters waiting to happen. Precautionary measures could reduce damage and save lives.

Slum formation is neither an inevitable consequence of urbanization, nor can it be solely blamed on a lack of financial resources. Slums are also produced by bad governance, failed policies, inappropriate legal and regulatory frameworks, corruption and lack of political will.

© Magnus Rosshagen

The current methods and definitions used for poverty measurement are not sufficiently developed to give accurate information on the scale and nature of urban poverty. As a consequence, Poverty Reduction Strategies do not address the issue appropriately.

Who are the poor?

Urban poverty is underestimated

Efforts to measure poverty in order to prepare poverty reduction strategies tend to underestimate the number of urban poor.

One reason is that homeless people, as well as people living in illegal settlements or cheap boarding houses are not registered and only partially covered by household surveys.

Another reason is that figures on income or provision of services too often are calculated as an average per capita for areas and populations, which include both poor and high-income groups. The difference between the rich and the poor is huge even in smaller towns and this urban phenomenon makes aggregate data irrelevant for poverty analysis.

The way poverty is measured and how poverty lines are defined and applied is perhaps the most critical factor. A simple monetary poverty line like 'one USD per day' will systematically underestimate the number of urban poor as well as the severity of urban poverty, since the urban poor live in a cash economy and have much higher (monetary) living costs than the rural poor. Sometimes poverty lines relate to the cost of a minimum food basket, or cost of the minimum calorie intake. While these are an improvement on the dollar per day measure, they disregard the high costs for non-food items and necessary services (like transport and energy) in urban areas. More sophisticated definitions count in 'non-food items'. Typically between 30 per cent and 80 per cent of the minimum food basket cost is added. However, this adjustment is based on very little empirical data and does not reflect living cost in larger cities, where transport fuel and housing costs are often much higher.

Poverty lines may in fact be set so low that even households living in tiny shacks built on pavements are not defined as poor. There are examples of statistics showing that only 1–15 per cent of an urban population is poor, while more specific data on housing conditions and deficiencies in infrastructure and service provision find that one-third or even one-half is living in poverty. In some nations with a low official level of urban poverty, the infant and child mortality rates are 10–20 times what would be expected in places with little poverty.

To broaden the definition of poverty, some Poverty Reduction Strategy Papers (PRSPs) also count in access to health, education, safe water and similar basic needs.[9] The distance to the service is usually used as indicator, and since urban distances are usually shorter, results seem to indicate a lower level of poverty. Proximity however, is not a sufficient criterion. A poor household in an urban area may be close to a standpipe, but delivery may be unreliable. When there is water, there may be a long queue, when there is none people are forced to buy from water vendors. Similarly, a slum area may be right next to an excellent hospital, but that does not mean that its medical services are available to the slum dwellers.

Other aspects of poverty are highly relevant for the urban poor. For example, the income poverty lines do not consider the asset bases, security of tenure, rule of law and respect for civil and political rights.

The shortcomings described above tend to underestimate urban poverty systematically. This is particularly the case for larger cities. The conclusion must be, that the methods and definitions used for poverty measurement are not sufficiently developed to give accurate information about the scale and nature of urban poverty. Because of the complex context and the huge inter-urban and intra-urban differentials, it is not possible to improve quality without more in-depth knowledge of the conditions of the urban poor. More field surveys and refined analysis are required, but also more participation from the civil society represented by CBOs and NGOs and other institutions – those actively working with the urban poor.

Urban poverty is increasing

The World Development Report 1999 suggested that there would be almost 500 million urban poor by 2000. A recent detailed review of the provision of water and sanitation indicates that 850 million people, 40 per cent of the urban population, currently lack one of these.

UN-HABITAT estimates that 43 per cent of the urban population in developing countries lives in slums, (see Table 4, p 54) in the least developed countries 78 per cent, and in the whole of Sub-Saharan Africa, 72 per cent. The UN-HABITAT definition of slum is a household lacking one of five indicators – water, sanitation, durable housing, living area with a maximum of 2 people per room and secure tenure. So far UN-HABITAT has only used the first four indicators since information about tenure is insufficient.

---

9) PRSPs are produced by the government of a developing country. Initially a requirement of the process to reduce the debt burden of Highly Indebted Poor Countries (HIPC), but has now become a general tool for the attainment of the Millennium Development Goals.

The urban poor seem to have increased as a percentage of the total urban population. This could be explained by macroeconomic factors such as economic decline in many countries, the 'Asian crisis' and the effects of structural economic reforms.

Except for the poorest and least urbanized countries, the proportion of urban poor may decrease in the future as a result of economic development together with better governance and pro-poor policies. Their total number will probably still continue to increase because of the growing population in urban areas. Rural poverty, on the other hand, would tend to decline in numbers but not necessarily as a share of the rural population.

Women and children are a majority of the poor

Poverty cannot be discussed only at the level of settlements or households. A woman or other household member may be poor, even in a family with assets and an acceptable income if the family resources are controlled and perhaps consumed by the husband or some other person. In urban areas many people survive as a single-person household, so it is misleading to discuss households as a homogeneous group. In this respect it is important to see to the needs of particularly vulnerable groups like the aged, the handicapped, single mothers and children. Of the poor, women are often the poorest, and it is the poorest women and their children who suffer most from lack of basic services and the hazards of life in the slums.

Many households are headed by women – for example 25 per cent of households in Honduras and 32 per cent in Honduran urban areas. Women-headed households are vulnerable but not always the poorest. A study of three district towns in Tanzania found that independent women with resources, such as farmland, capital or skills, were better off than their married counterparts.[10] The explanation is that married women may have to surrender their income to their husbands, or their husbands perhaps do not allow them to earn an income of their own.

Extended households with numerous dependants including old persons and young mothers who cannot survive on their own are vulnerable too. Single mothers are in a difficult situation, no matter what their circumstances are.

The HIV/AIDS pandemic has had devastating effects and young women are disproportionately affected. Beside the likelihood of being infected, nursing the sick is mostly a task for women and young girls. This means that girls in areas with high prevalence of HIV/AIDS often have to leave school to take over the housekeeping or nursing.

---

10) Baker and Mwaiselage (1993)

Poor women often have to earn their income through 'survival activities' such as petty trading, prostitution and small-scale agriculture. Women also run micro-enterprises involving market trading, restaurants, bars, brewing beer, shops, bakeries, sewing and mending clothes. In many countries, the informal economy, especially the 'bottom end' with lowest returns, is a female economy (see also Table 3).

The children of the poor also have to earn money at a young age in the informal economy. Much of this work is risky, both physically and socially. For women working outside their homes, day care for their children is a major problem. For this and for economic reasons female-headed micro-businesses are often home-based. Women carry the major burden of productive, reproductive and community managing work. As main stake-holders at the primary level they are then the key to progress, and any programme to address the needs of the poor has to incorporate the women. This does not mean that men should be left out, but it is critical that women be involved in decision-making from the beginning and throughout the entire process.

Also important, but less noticed, is the need to involve youth. Unemployed young people are a potential resource, but at the same time a potential threat to society. Without meaningful occupation they may slip into crime, drug abuse or become involved in gangs or in extreme and destructive political or religious sects.

Most of the urban poor earn their living in the informal economy. Many are self-employed, but the informal economy also comprises a great number of persons with wage employment.

Earning a living

'Formal' and 'informal' economies

Most of the urban poor (and many of the better off) earn their living in the 'informal economy' or 'informal sector'. It is the 'economy of the poor' but a vital sector of the economy as well and thus significant both from an economic and a social point of view.

The informal economy covers all sorts of activities and there is no sharp line between 'formal' and 'informal'. A generally adopted definition is that a registered business is formal – the rest informal. This distinction, however, does not help much when it comes to analysing the nature of the economic activities from which the poor earn their livelihood. This is the focus here and the term 'informal economy/sector' is used for micro-scale business activities whether registered or not.

The informal economy comprises at one end of the scale the self-employed producing only survival level earnings and at the other end viable micro-enterprises with several employees. As they grow, they will be classified as small enterprises and perhaps enter the 'formal economy'. What looks at first sight to be small and informal, may actually be part of a bigger (formal or informal) business scheme – for instance when wealthy persons invest in rickshaws for lease.

Many people with a formal job earn additional money from informal business. The household economy is often based on both formal and informal earnings.

The informal economy is very competitive. It is possible to earn a lot of money – more than from formal employment, but most people involved are not that successful.

It is difficult to estimate the volume of the informal economy. Some studies claim that, at least in some countries, it employs more than half of the total workforce, and that its contribution to GDP is around 30 per cent in Latin America and Asia and 40 per cent in Sub-Saharan Africa.[11] The World Bank has estimated that in many Sub-Saharan countries the informal economy accounts for as much as two-thirds of urban employment.

Workshop specializing in cooking appliances: pots and pans, water containers and charcoal stoves. Everything is made from scratch with quite simple tools. Most urban poor earn their living from micro-scale businesses in the informal economy, which also provide them with commodities and services at affordable prices.

© Heldur Netocny / PHOENIX

11) Flodman Becker, Kristina (2004) *The Informal Economy, Fact finding study*, Sida, Stockholm.

Table 3. The size of the informal economy and its components

	Total	Women	Men	Self-employed	Wage employed
SIZE OF THE INFORMAL ECONOMY (Share of non-agricultural employment)				**COMPONENTS OF THE INFORMAL ECONOMY**	
Sub-Saharan Africa	72%	84%	63%	70%	30%
Asia	65%	65%	65%	59%	41%
Latin America	51%	58%	48%	60%	40%

Source: ILO, Geneva 2002. *Women and Men in the Informal Economy*.

This is confirmed by ILO (Table 3), and data show that the informal economy is an important source of income for women.[12] Table 3 also shows, that although the self-employed dominate, the informal economy generates a lot of wage employment too – a fact which is sometimes overlooked.

The informal economy is not a new phenomenon, it is indeed the original urban economy: small scale crafts, services and trade are the traditional business of towns.

Micro-enterprises remain informal because access to the formal economy can be difficult and expensive. The procedures to get permits or land titles are cumbersome. Bribes are often required, taxes and other fees have to be paid.

The informal economy needs to be regarded from several angles. It is a significant development factor. For the urban poor it offers jobs and income. It includes emerging enterprises and at the same time very poor women struggling to feed the family. However, it is not only a matter of income generation. An important aspect is that many essential services and commodities at affordable prices for low-income households are only produced in this sector.

Urban agriculture

Urban agriculture is a source of food and additional income for many urban poor, but also includes highly commercialised operations.

Urban agriculture in this second sense may focus on high yield production of vegetables, fruit, fish, small livestock like rabbits and chicken and supplementary products like berries, nuts, herbs and species, but even staples such as cassava, maize and beans may also be grown. These farmers are not from the poorest groups. Their contribution to agricultural production and to local economies is substantial

For the urban poor and women in particular, small scale agriculture pro-

---

12) ILO (2002) *Women and Men in the Informal Economy* . International Labour Organization, Geneva.

vides some food security and additional income. Low demand on capital and know-how are advantages. Lack of land is the main constraint, but another constraint is that urban agriculture is banned in many cities. The extent of urban agriculture varies: in times of economic crisis it tends to increase and in Sub-Saharan Africa it has grown rapidly as an informal activity over the past 15 years. In smaller rural towns, especially but not exclusively in Africa, agriculture is a common complement to other sources of income. Small-scale urban agriculture may be insignificant in economic terms, but it is a livelihood option for the urban poor.

In spite of the advantages, city regulations often restrict urban agriculture because it could pose health risks. These risks are particularly related to animal husbandry in densely populated settlements, but restrictions are often unnecessarily rigid and could be better adapted to local conditions.

Urban agriculture offers environmental advantages too. Nutrients that are brought to the city population can be recycled, especially if combined with ecological sanitation which returns the nutrients in human excreta to the soil (Box 15, p 104).

FURTHER READING

Mitlin, Diana (2004) *Understanding urban poverty; what the poverty Reduction Strategy Papers tell us,* Poverty Reduction in Urban Areas Series,Working Paper 13, IIED, London

Satterthwaite, David (2004) *The under-estimation of urban poverty in low and middle-income nation,* Poverty Reduction in Urban Areas Series,Working Paper 14, IIED, London

ILO (2002) *Women and men in the informal economy – A statistical picture,* International Labour Organization, Geneva

UNDP (1996) *Urban Agriculture: Food, Jobs and Sustainable Cities,* United Nations Development Programme, New York

3. CITIES AND TOWNS FACING PROBLEMS

Urbanization, per se, is not a problem – it brings benefits, but these are not equally distributed and the rapid growth of urban centres is accompanied by serious problems. However, the economic, social and cultural environments in an urban centre obviously do bring benefits, hope and opportunities – even for the poor.

UN-HABITAT estimates that close to 900 million people live in slum areas lacking basic services. If present trends continue, there will be more than 1.4 billion slum dwellers by 2020. For the urban poor, the house is often more than a home, it is also a workplace. The lack of basic services not only causes human suffering but also reduces productivity and income.

Slums, favelas, shantytowns

Poor housing conditions

Governments in the developing world cannot cope with unprecedented urban growth. The most visible signs of failure are the mushrooming slum areas, where the lack of the most basic infrastructure can make the provision of social services, such as health care, ineffectual. Similarly, the lack of infrastructure increases the cost to the poor of necessities, such as water, energy and transport, and reduces productivity and economic opportunities both in the formal and informal economy.

The issue of housing is obviously not only a matter of houses, but includes the basic infrastructure of a neighbourhood as well as schools, clinics, religious buildings, sports grounds and other amenities. The individual dwelling is important, but water, sanitation, electricity, access roads, lighting, transportation, etc are indispensable complements. The quality of houses is usually very poor in urban slums, but other shortages are often more serious, since these are dependent on external factors. Poor people have neither the means to improve the situation by their own efforts nor the power to influence the responsible authorities. Typical are the lack of basic infrastructure, unreliable services, as well as insecure and non-formalized land tenure. The problem of urban slums is thus multidimensional. Any solution would require a combination of technical, financial and legal interventions. Different types of action are required for improvements in housing (a private good) and infrastructure (a public good). The public sector has a responsibility to provide basic infrastructure, while housing is a matter of enabling people to themselves improve their conditions.

Poor and overcrowded housing in densely populated urban areas contributes to the transmission of diseases including tuberculosis (TB). TB is among the leading causes of death for adults in developing countries. The interaction between HIV and TB and the spread of drug-resistant forms of TB have led to a resurgence of the disease in many places, including the transition countries. Many disease vectors are linked to poor quality hous-

Table 4. Regional distribution of the world's urban slum dwellers. (2001)

Region	Total urban population (thousands)	% slum dwellers
Sub-Saharan Africa	231 052	71.9
Asia Pacific	1 211 540	43.2
Latin America and Caribbean	399 385	31.9
Middle East, and North Africa	145 624	29.5
Transition economies	259 091	9.6
Advanced economies	676 492	5.8
World	2 921 184	31.6
Developing countries	2 021 665	43
Least developed countries	179 239	78.2

Source: UN-HABITAT, *The State of the World's Cities*, 2004/2005.

ing (Chagas disease) or inadequate water management (malaria, dengue, yellow fever). The health burden and premature death caused by inadequate provision of water and sanitation is discussed in 'Environment and health' (p 62).

Crowded and cramped conditions also increase the number of accidents in the home. especially where open fires are still used. Smoke from fires and stoves is a serious health risk, especially for those who spend most time at the hearth, usually women and small children.

Two circumstances make housing a priority issue for women. Firstly, it is women who take responsibility for home and children – sometimes alone. Secondly, it is mostly women who run home-based enterprises. A house then is not only a home but also a means of income generation. Part of the home could be a small shop or kiosk, or used for sewing and mending dresses, weaving, basket making or whatever. Manufacturing at home for someone who supplies the raw materials and pays for the products is a common source of income. Beside space, a reliable supply of electricity and water is essential. City planners rarely take these requirements of home-based enterprises into account.

Lack of secure tenure

Forced evictions are becoming more frequent and the lack of security of tenure is a major problem for a large number of urban dwellers and an obstacle to economic development.

In the developing world, it can be almost impossible, for poor urban dwellers to own or rent with any reasonable degree of security of tenure. The reasons for this lack of security are many, and are the result of how the

A 'street' in Kibera, Nairobi. Poor housing, no infrastructure and lack of basic services. No wonder infant mortality is very high (see Table 2).

© Sean Sprague/Phoenix

We share a belief in the democratic future of this country and the right of every South African to the dignity and inner peace which can be gained from a house which can be called a home.

But we need to share too the understanding of how urgent it is that we redouble our efforts to get the housing right. We will not be able to fully assert our democratic rights in this country, we will not be able to form the communities which are essential to a stable and democratic country if we do not get the issue of housing right.

Housing is a physical requirement. But it is also much more – it is a spiritual need, which goes to the root of a dignified and tolerable life. It is at the core of a better life for all South Africans.

The late Joe Slovo, the first Minister of Housing
in South Africa after the end of the apartheid regime

poor or their landlords had taken possession of the land and erected the dwellings in the first place. Was it spontaneous squatting on public or private land, or organized large-scale invasion of public land, or was it unauthorized housing on agricultural land bought from the farmer?

Obsolete zoning regulations and building codes requiring unaffordable construction methods and housing standards are obstacles to formal recognition. People also refrain from formal status because high transfer taxes and complicated procedures make it difficult and costly to register the purchase of a property. In many cities the authorities refuse to provide basic services to those who lack title to their property. Insecure tenure reduces the incentives for poor urban households (or their landlords) to invest in housing improvements (Box 6).

Tenure security, is not solely a matter of having a legal title to land. Property sales often occur in informal settlements despite the lack of full legal documentation and there are several measures short of obtaining legal title that can improve security. Some residents of informal settlements have ownership rights – they have bought the plot; while others are squatters in constant fear of eviction. Residents often see the provision of basic utilities as providing de facto security of tenure, which in turn encourages investment in house improvements. People are often willing to contribute labour and even money to get access to services because they believe that this will improve their security.

Forced evictions are unfortunately becoming more frequent. Four mil-

Mzee Osman Kur, a successful micro-entrepreneur, has lived all 68 years of his life in the Kibera informal settlement in Nairobi. His family claims they were granted the land by the British colonial government, but never given formal title, despite government promises since 1964.

The Mzee plot is well developed, with several one-room units on the front of the plot rented to businesses, and a separate structure where Mzee, three generations of his family, and several tenants live. Despite the length of time Mzee and his family have occupied the land and his relative success as a micro-entrepreneur, all of the buildings on the plot are wattle and daub walls plastered with cement.

Although he could afford to invest in more permanent structures, Mzee explains, 'I am not willing to invest too much in putting up stone structures because I can be evicted from here any time. I still do not have title to my land.' Mzee and his family continue to make attempts to acquire their title, but there is no clear process to be followed and the local chief has expressed little interest in responding to Mzee's requests.

Quoted from ACCION and CFH International 2002

lion people were evicted during the period 1998–2000 and 6.7 million between 2001 and 2002.[13]

The issue of secure tenure and protection against forced eviction usually refers to home ownership. Less attention has been paid to the situation of tenants. There are different categories of tenants: some are lodgers who can only afford to rent a small space – perhaps shared with others – in a private home, and some live in extremely crowded blocks of flats. None have legal protection. These are often the poorest of the urban poor.

The National Bureau of Statistics of Tanzania estimates that about 55 per cent of the households in Dar es Salaam are private sector tenants, while only about 6 per cent are tenants in public housing. In other urban centres the corresponding figures were 36 per cent and 2 per cent respectively.[14] Other studies maintain that the majority of urban Tanzanians are tenants in the informal settlements.[15]

In many countries there is no legislation on tenancy rights. When such legislation exists, it is in most cases obsolete. The idea was to keep rents down, but the result has often been that landlords cannot cover the costs and have been forced to refrain from badly needed repair and maintenance. However, legal protection of tenancy rights is indispensable and would benefit the poorest of the urban poor. The vulnerability of this

---

13) COHRE (2002) *Global survey 8, Forced Evictions, Violation of Human Rights*, Centre on Housing Rights and Evictions, Geneva
14) Household survey 2000/2001
15) International Union of Tenants (2005) *Global Tenant*, Aug 2005, IUT, Stockholm

group calls for support institutions, which could help people to settle conflicts and claim legal rights. In South Africa an organization of this type has been very effective. Associations of tenants could take on this task and play an advocacy role as well.

For women, working from the home and responsible for their children, secure tenure is particularly important. Secure tenure is more important than formal ownership. Ones own house, however, is an important asset and reduces the vulnerability of a poor household.

Many developing countries have adopted laws that establish equal rights for men and women with respect to ownership and heritage of property. Unfortunately, these laws are not always respected. Women may not even be aware of their rights. The need to protect the rights of widows has been accentuated in a tragic way due to the death toll of HIV/AIDS, and 'property grabbing' by the husband's relatives is not unusual.

Indian slum dwellers live in hutments near a water pipeline in India's financial capital Mumbai.

© Punit Paranjpe/Scanpix

The land issue

Serviced land for new housing is rarely available or affordable for the poor. Often they have no choice but to settle wherever there is vacant land on the outskirts of the town. There is no infrastructure, and transport to town is cumbersome and costly. Alternatively, and in order to live closer to job opportunities, the poor may occupy more centrally located pieces of land left over because they were not suitable for housing. These could be along the railway track, on steep slopes or in ravines, on rubbish dumps, or in other dangerous or unhealthy places. Living on steep slopes is hazardous and landslides have often destroyed settlements and killed many people. In Tegucigalpa, the capital of Honduras, the heavy rain of hurricane Mitch caused a major landslide, which eliminated an entire settlement and buried many of its inhabitants.

The reason why the poor cannot find a place to build is rarely because there is a real shortage of suitable land. Cities on islands and in hilly areas face physical constraints of course, but in most other cases land is abundant. The failure is rather due to poor governance, an inappropriate institutional framework and non-functioning land markets. In some countries authorities try to discourage migration and deliberately limit access to land and services for new housing.

'Only bankers can get mortgages'

In most developing countries formal housing finance institutions (banks, building societies, savings and loans or cooperative institutions, etc) play only a limited role in meeting the housing needs of the urban poor or even of the middle class. In Uganda, for example, only 200 mortgage loans are issued yearly, although about 50.000 new urban dwellings are built. In Kenya, the total stock of outstanding mortgage loans is about 30.000 and less than 5 per cent of new urban dwellings are constructed with the benefit of a mortgage. In Nairobi people joke: 'Only bankers can get mortgages'.

Compared to other low-income countries, India has a developed housing finance industry. More than 80 private housing finance institutions have been established during the last decade, some of which rely on refinancing from the National Housing Bank. They also respond to incentives that form part of India's system of directed lending. But even with this relatively advanced financial sector, only 22 per cent of new homes are financed with a mortgage, and it is mainly the upper and upper-middle income groups that qualify for loans.

Macro-economic policies influence the performance of housing finance systems. Zambia, for example, has a fairly well developed banking sector compared to other low-income Sub-Saharan countries. However, the government has largely crowded out private sector borrowers. High inflation and high real interest rates have virtually obliterated the long-term debt market. This is especially the case for the housing finance market. In 2003, Zambia's three mortgage lending institutions had total assets of about USD 10 million, of which only 15 per cent had been transformed into mortgages.

The formal housing finance lenders prefer clients with a steady income and properties with registered titles. Since the majority of slum dwellers are employed in the informal sector their incomes are undocumented, and they may not be able to show evidence of income or formal title. For many the main constraint is, at any rate, that income is too low or too variable. Even in high-income nations, those with low or variable incomes find it hard to qualify for mortgage finance.

Most housing finance institutions also consider the transaction costs for loans to the urban poor to be high compared to the loan amounts. Furthermore, their staff generally are unfamiliar with the social and economic circumstances of low-income urban households, and not trained to deal with them.

Basic services

The provision of water and sanitation in low-income areas is worse than is generally assumed. Statistics are based on number of connected households, but do not tell whether the pipe actually delivers water. Field studies during the 1990s revealed that the infrastructure for poor people had declined, and communities which received piped water during the 1970s had serious supply problems 20 years later, due to poor maintenance and inefficient management.

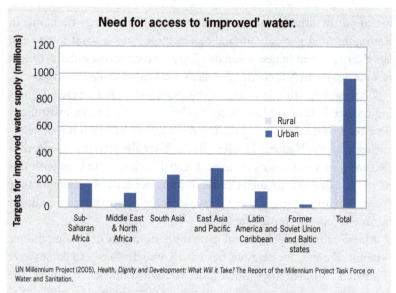

Need for access to 'improved' water.

FIGURE 7
The figure shows the number of rural and urban dwellers that must gain access to 'improved' water supply between 2002 and 2015 if MDG Target 10 is to be met.

The cost of water is typically subsidized. This favours the more wealthy with piped connections and a more reliable supply. Big consumers like state owned companies and public institutions frequently do not even pay their water bills. The poorest, who are rarely connected, do not benefit from the subsidies and have to buy water by the bucket from vendors. These private water vendors have typically been seen as profiting from the poor. In fact they provide an important service – often the sole alternative available, and cannot be blamed for the deficient public service.

The coverage of infrastructure systems is highly unequal. In Lagos only 6 per cent of households have their own connections; in Lusaka, 10 per cent; and i Nairobi, 12 per cent. Piped water may be available in theory, but the distribution of water is often irregular and many low-income areas are located outside the network. A number of studies suggest that poor people spend 10 per cent of their income on the direct costs of informally vended water. Hygiene requires sufficient quantities of clean water. However, the

Table 5. Urban population without adequate water and sanitation in 2000.

Region	Water	Sanitation
Africa	35–50%	50–60%
Asia	35–50%	45–60%

UN-HABITAT (2002). *Water and Sanitation in the World's Cities: Local Action for Global Goals*, Earthscan, London

cost of water may be prohibitive. A study in Central America revealed that households with water connections used 29.3 cubic metres per month compared to 5.5 for those without piped water.[16] The cost was USD 14.6 per month for those with piped water but USD 20.8 per month for those without. This means that those not connected used only about a quarter of the amount of those connected, had to pay 7.5 times more per cubic meter, and their monthly cost for much less water was higher.

Piped sewerage systems are rarely available in low-income areas, and people have to invest in their own sanitation solutions. Pit latrines are the most common solution, but these also bring problems such as flooding, overfilling and ground water pollution. Affordable and safe sanitation solutions for urban areas are rare, especially when the population density or a rocky ground make pit latrines impossible.

Electricity is more often generally available – even to poor neighbourhoods; in Latin America the poorest squatter areas are serviced. This is partly explained by lower connection costs for electricity, but also by more effective commercial management ensuring cost recovery and the payment of electricity bills. In some places pre-payment systems are used.

Access roads are usually bad, and within the neighbourhood itself there are often no roads at all, no storm water drainage and no retaining walls against erosion. This makes the settlements vulnerable to earthquakes, landslides and flooding with serious consequences. Unfortunately, these unsafe conditions often are found even in planned settlements. As for solid waste collection, marginal areas are rarely served, and refuse is dumped or burned exacerbating drainage problems and adding to unsanitary conditions.

---

16) Walker, Ian, Ordonez, Fidel, Serrano, Pedro and Halpern, Jonathan (2004) *Pricing, Subsidies and the Poor: Demand for Improved Water Services in Central America*, Policy Research Working Paper 2468, World Bank, Washington

"The environmental burdens of poverty are suffered by the poor and dealt with by the poor. The environmental burdens of affluence are suffered by the public and dealt with by the government".[17]
The poor suffer from a double burden since they can escape neither the one nor the other.

Environment and health

The environmental 'footprint' – a misleading concept?

Urban centres in developing countries – just like those in the North – are sources of pollution and consumers of natural resources. The environmental burden is determined by three urban features: *consumption patterns, industrialization and concentration.*

Growing upper and middle classes in urban areas consume energy, produce waste and use cars. Industries pollute air, water and soil. The concentration of traffic, industries and people in urban areas does mean a concentration of waste and pollution, but not necessarily more pollution or resource use than if the same activities and people were dispersed. Problems occur when the pollution level is too high, when the surroundings cannot sustainably satisfy the needs for water, energy, or raw materials for example, and if the reuse of scarce resources is hindered, such as for phosphorus (see 'Global and regional impacts', p 65). On the other hand, urban concentration also makes it easier to address many problems.

It is economic development, not urbanization, which is the cause of the additional environmental burdens. In this sense, the wide-spread 'footprint' concept could be misleading, since it focuses on the spatial dimension. The 'footprint' shows the extension of the environmental impact from an urban agglomeration and is used to illustrate how far this impact goes in terms of pollution and exploitation of the natural resources. This makes it seem that the city is the culprit: 'without cities - no footprint'. But it is 'the foot of development' that leaves the print; and economic development cannot take place without cities.

To address the challenges, environmental management needs a correct understanding of causes and impacts and should focus on the aspects of production and consumption patterns, which are the cause of environmental degradation. Obviously, this is still an urban issue, and it is in the urban areas where many and perhaps the most serious environmental challenges have to

Scavengers on a burning garbage dump. The collection and re-use of waste provides a livelihood for many urban poor and is basically positive, but working conditions are unhealthy. Old dumps need to be relocated and managed in order to protect the environment and offer safe working conditions.

© Sean Sprague / PHOENIX

---

17) Marianne Kjellén, Stockholm Environment Institute (SEI).

be met – in the words of the executive director of UNEP, Mr. Claus Töpfer in his speech at the World Environment Day in San Francisco in 2005: "The battle for a clean environment will be lost or won in cities".

Most serious are local health impacts

The most critical immediate urban environmental problems in poor developing countries are not global warming or the regional impacts of pollution, but the local environmental health issues related to the lack of safe drinking water and of proper sanitation (Box 7). Water, sanitation, drainage, solid waste and local air pollution are commonly referred to as the 'brown agenda'.

It is poor people, children and women in particular, who suffer. In total more than four million people in urban and rural areas die each year from diarrhoeal diseases, linked to contaminated food or water, inadequate sanitation and lack of hygiene. Child mortality for the urban poor is often as high as for rural children, and can be even higher – as for Nairobi (Table 2, p 40).

Poor quality housing in densely populated urban areas contributes to large health burdens and premature death. Overcrowded housing increases the transmission of infectious diseases.

Again there are marked differences between poor and wealthy areas in the same city. A study in Accra, Ghana, on environmental problems at household level for different types of residential areas found a clear correlation between ill-health and low income: This was explained by deficient housing and unsanitary neighbourhood environments.

In order to live closer to sources of income and avoid time and costs for

---

Box 7: Environmental problems at the neighbourhood level

In poor cities, and especially their poor neighbourhoods, environmental problems tend to stay close to home. This is particularly true in the Third World. Inadequate household water supplies are typically more critical to people's wellbeing than contaminated waterways. Air pollution in the kitchen is often far worse than outdoors. Waste accumulating in the neighbourhood commonly raises more serious problems than at the city dumps. Human excreta is frequently the most critical pollutant, and unsanitary conditions at home are generally a more immediate threat than industrial pollution. City-wide environmental problems can also be severe in low-income cities, but only rarely cause as much human hardship as those at the household and neighbourhood level. Moreover, while the burden of most environmental problems falls more heavily on the poor, household and neighbourhood problems are especially selective, with poor women and children bearing an inordinate share of the burden.

Gordon McGranahan, International Institute for Environment and Development, IIED

transportation, the poor often settle on better located pieces of land, left vacant because they were unsuitable for building and exposed to environmental dangers. The consequences of the accident at the Union Carbide chemical plant in Bhopal became very serious because squatter settlements were right up against the perimeter fence.

Air pollution caused by traffic, industry and cooking fires may locally reach health-threatening levels. According to WHO, 800 000 deaths per year are due to air pollution, two-thirds of these in Asia.

The environment agenda tends to highlight the environmental threats to the rich nations or the wealthy elite in developing countries while it is the urban poor in these countries who face the most serious and multiple burdens. Many live in unhealthy environments characterised by a complex of interrelated risks involving crowding, sanitary hazards, unsafe or insufficient water, indoor air pollution, accumulation of waste and disease-bearing pests. At the same time they live in areas also threatened by 'modern' risks, the result of industrialization and motorization. The poor also share the threat of global risks such as climate change consequences.

Global and regional impacts

So far cities in poor countries in the South have contributed less to global environmental problems than urban areas in the North. Their consumption of energy and non-renewable natural resources has been low because they are poor. Heating is rarely required, and air conditioning and private car ownership is limited. Air pollution from cooking fires and diesel engines is serious, however. So is water pollution. The impact has mostly been limited to the local or regional environment.

This pattern is changing. Many countries – particularly in Asia and Latin America – now experience rapid economic growth with the more prosperous tending to adopt the consumption patterns of the North. This will contribute to global environmental problems. Even less successful countries have a growing modern sector. The size of this rich and modern sector should not be underestimated. The richest 10 per cent in India represent more people than the entire population of England or France and the richest 10 per cent in Nigeria more than the whole population of Sweden. The number of Chinese households with similar economic conditions is even higher. And most of these richer people live in the major cities. The environmental impact of their consumption may compare with countries in the North, and is growing rapidly.

Politicians, producers and consumers in these emerging economies may not be very sensitive to the environmental challenge, technologies are not always 'clean'; poor maintenance increases pollution; and efficiency in energy use is low. The laws are usually there, but enforcement and monitoring suffer from weak institutional capacity and widespread corruption.

Cities in developing countries can have a substantial impact on the surrounding region. A few examples are given below:

Many cities are located by a sea, a lake or a river. Pollution of the water is a health hazard for the local population and may lead to depletion of fish, which might be their main (or only) source of primary protein. Large coastal cities have an adverse effect on aquatic life, including coastal ecosystems and may, for instance, destroy coral reefs.

The cutting of fuel-wood and the production of charcoal may lead to deforestation, which in turn causes erosion, landslides and floods. These may also affect the city.

Urban centres also cut or disturb natural circuits for various substances. The case of phosphorus is crucial. Phosphorus is a limited resource with an unsustainable linear flow from ore to fertiliser; then consumed in food it passes through the body, is carried through waterborne sanitation systems and finally is lost in the sea – where it is a pollutant.

Shortage of fresh water is often mentioned by environmentalists as a 'killing factor' for urban centres. In fact household consumption is rather low, particularly in poor communities. The quantity required to meet basic needs is about 20 litres per capita per day. This is only a fraction of the water delivered by municipalities. The major water consumers are agriculture and industry and this is where conservation could have the greatest effect. Golf courses and garden lawns use a lot too.

Weak urban governance, insufficient municipal resources, inadequate infrastructure, distorted land and housing markets and inappropriate regulatory frameworks are obstacles to sustainable urban development. The consequences of the HIV/AIDS pandemic cannot be overlooked.

Development obstacles

Weak urban governance

Good urban governance is rare, and reforms are needed in most developing countries. Urban policies at the central level are generally inadequate or absent, and legal frameworks inappropriate. The distribution of responsibility and authority between different levels of government is ineffective and the fiscal system in need of reform. Central governments often retain control over revenues and expenses and even of municipal services like water supply, electricity and transport. This hardly promotes local development.

Financial resources and institutional capacity at all levels are very limited. Planning, infrastructure development, service provision and other responsibilities obviously suffer from lack of human resources – especially at the local level.

Good governance is a political issue more than a 'technical' matter of efficiency in public administration. A fundamental problem is the unequal power structure of the society. Even when local authorities are democratically elected, which is not always the case, the political and economic power remains in the hands of an elite with vested interests. The allocation of scarce resources like service provision is too often characterised by corruption and 'clientalism'. The poor have little or no opportunities to make their voice heard and are rarely represented in government. Governments – central and local – generally regard civil society with suspicion and even hostility and contempt. The prevalent political structure does not appear to support the development of long term pro-poor policies.

Fragile democracy, nepotism, corruption and lack of transparency are fundamental obstacles to development in general and not only to urban governance. But in spite of all these weaknesses the democratically elected local authority is the primary governance institution for urban areas, and to achieve the potential for sustainable urban development these weaknesses must be addressed.

Poor municipalities

The provision of basic services and local infrastructure is supposed to be the domain of municipal governments. In reality, however, it is only municipalities in Eastern Europe and in the former Soviet Union that fulfil their responsibilities in the same way as in OECD countries. In the Middle East, North Africa and Sub-Saharan Africa, municipalities are marginal actors, generally accounting for less than one-twentieth of all public expenditures. In Asia and Latin America municipalities – especially in the middle-income countries – have somewhat greater capabilities and resources.

Many countries have sought to decentralize service delivery to local governments – without providing the necessary financial means however.

Consequently, in most developing countries, transfers from central (or provincial/state) governments make up a significant share of municipal revenues. Still, in most developing countries, municipalities account for only a minor share of public expenditures. Local government's share of total government revenues and expenditures for a number of countries is shown in Table A11 (Annexes, p 178).

In most low-income countries, municipal investment budgets are extremely limited. The Lusaka City Council, for example, has an annual investment budget of around USD 1.50 per inhabitant. The corresponding figure for Douala is around USD 2.00. Central governments tend to finance and build all major infrastructure, leaving local governments responsible for such marginal activities as solid waste collection, bus terminals and slaughterhouses. As can be seen from Figure 8, this is a common situation.

Municipal budgets often require approval from central government. In Tanzania, for example, central government approves all municipal budgets and determines the amount of transfers based on what the municipalities can raise on their own. (Thus, improved local revenue is punished through

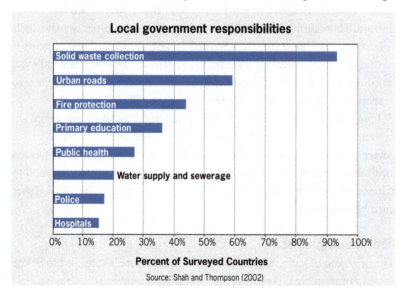

Local government responsibilities

Source: Shah and Thompson (2002)

FIGURE 8.
The tasks of the local authorities are often very limited. The graph is based on a sample of 36 developing countries.

reduced transfers.) Central government would need to approve any long-term borrowing by municipalities and its approval is often perceived as a guarantee that sufficient funding would be available for servicing the debt.

Central governments control all major revenue sources; municipalities are left with just a few 'nuisance taxes' – in Senegal, for example, more than 300 different fees and business taxes.

Although local governments depend on transfers from central government, most countries do not have a rational, transparent system for fund allocation. Transfers tend to be determined by political considerations. They vary from year to year, which makes it impossible to plan any large-scale infrastructure investments requiring several years of capital outlays. However, in a few countries, the situation is different: in Bolivia, an automatic transfer system ensures that the local governments receive 20 per cent of all central government revenues.

Statutory restrictions on municipal borrowing frequently preclude this option. The reason may be that government wants to control or limit public sector debt, or is afraid that local authorities will borrow excessively in the expectation that the state will bail them out anyway. Municipalities in Sri Lanka have the legal right to borrow and to issue bonds, but since the Municipal Ordinance does not allow them to pledge assets or revenue streams as security, in practice they are prevented from accessing financing from banks and markets.

Even where municipalities do carry out and finance their own projects, commercial lenders are extremely cautious. Municipalities lack credit-worthiness due to the generally poor fiscal and regulatory framework and their lack of capacity for local revenue generation.

Inadequate infrastructure

In many cities in Africa and to some extent in Asia, infrastructure has not changed much since colonial times. Large areas are not covered due to lack of investment and the systems have deteriorated because maintenance has been neglected.

Inadequate infrastructure is a major obstacle for the development of the urban economy, and traffic congestion, communication problems and irregular supply of water and power seriously reduce productivity.

Detailed surveys in 1996 showed that manufacturing enterprises were frequently forced to invest in standby generators and their own wells (Table 6). In Lagos 92 per cent of the enterprises surveyed had their own generators and 44 per cent their own bore-holes. Those unable to afford such investments had to live with frequent disruptions in production. In Thailand, where public electric utilities are efficiently run, only 6 per cent had

Table 6. Firms with own wells and generators.

Poor infrastructure forces companies to invest in own solutions, which increases production costs.

COUNTRY	Firms with own wells/boreholes		Firms with own generators	
	% of firms	Cost (USD/m³)	% of firms	Cost (USD/kWh)
Nigeria	44%	25.8	92%	0.69
Indonesia	60%	0.86	65%	2.14
Thailand	24%	2.40	5%	n.a.

Source: Kyu Sik Lee and associates (1996).

private generators, but 24 per cent still needed a private water supply. The additional cost was considerable and at the same time these investments were under-utilized, operating at only 25–50 per cent of capacity. The costs of infrastructure deficiencies generally were more severe for small firms, the main source of employment growth in most developing countries.

A recent World Bank study for Uganda reached similar conclusions (Reinikka and Svensson, 1999). The respondents ranked poor utility services as a severe constraint to new investments, more severe than high taxes, poor tax administration, high interest rates, lack of access to finance, corruption, and the cost of raw materials.

Infrastructure deficiencies increase costs in several ways. To reduce the risk of supply interruption, manufacturers in developing countries feel obliged to keep raw material inventories that might be two to three times higher than in the United States (Guasch and Kogan, 2003). Real interest rates, which are at least twice as high, make the burden of excessive inventories worse for the industry.

As economic and trade reforms lower protective barriers and expose firms in developing countries to increased global competition, the quality of urban infrastructure will become even more significant. In many of the rapidly growing economies in East Asia, direct foreign investments and global competition are creating new patterns of development in the form of extended urban regions.

Distorted land and housing markets

There are active property markets in every city of the developing world. This is true even for the slums. A room is rented out, or a bed, or even just a space. Land and houses are bought and sold. Money is borrowed and lent. However, these markets tend to be highly segmented and distorted resulting in inflated prices and certainly do not work in favour of the poor

Traffic jam in Dhaka's Motijheel business district in Bangladesh. Inadequate infrastructure causes traffic congestion, communication problems and irregular water and power supplies, thus increasing production costs in many ways – a major obstacle for economic development.

© Mufty Munir/AFP-Scanpix

(Box 9). With the encouragement of the donor community, most governments have curtailed the construction of public housing and put their faith in the functioning of markets and private initiatives. Unfortunately, with few exceptions, governments have only paid lip service to the need to create an 'enabling environment' for increased investments in low-income housing and related infrastructure. A key constraint in this respect is the lack of secure tenure for the poor in most developing cities, which creates a segmented market and discourages housing investments.

Most countries have not amended the laws, regulations, policies and procedures that prevent land, housing and financial markets from working to the benefit of the poor rather than various powerful vested interests.

In Nairobi, for example, most of the city's low-income families are tenants or lodgers in overcrowded slums. The landlords are often politicians, bureaucrats or others with political influence. The rents are high enough to give these landlords 150 per cent annual returns on their 'investment' in a few shacks. In theory, such huge profits should lead to an increased supply of cheap housing. In practice, the investment is risky: occasional ruthless enforcement of zoning and building regulations has limited the supply of land and, thus, housing for the poor.

Inappropriate regulatory framework

The growth of slum settlements is often caused by inappropriate policy and regulatory frameworks, that push up the cost of land and housing for the poor. In his much acclaimed book, *The Other Path* (1989), de Soto argues that people operate in the informal market because they cannot afford 'formality'. He provides a case study of some of the problems causing the emergence of informal settlements. In Lima, Peru, the cost of adjudicating public land (the main source of vacant land for development in the city) and receiving approvals for urbanization plans, building and occupancy permits was a process that could take seven years. The cost (including bribes) could be more than USD 2 000 (in a country with a per capita income of around USD 600 at the time). This situation is in no way unique to Peru (where drastic improvements have been undertaken recently).

Zoning regulations for much of Nairobi mandate minimum plot sizes for single family dwellings of 2 000 sq m, and in some areas, 10 000 sq m. At the same time, almost 60 per cent of the city's population live in slums occupying perhaps 5 per cent of the urban area. Densities there can be as high as 15–20 persons per 100 square meters. Building codes require that a house have at least two rooms, be of stone, and have a separate cooking area, with flue ventilation. A low-income household might strive to achieve this standard over time, but such incremental building is illegal. In short, a 'legal' plot of land and a dwelling that meets building codes (following cumbersome approval procedures) is simply unaffordable. Large plot sizes also drive up costs. Providing infrastructure for 10,000 sq m plots costs roughly 10 times as much as for 100 sq m plots. To regulate against incremental building is particularly detrimental for the urban poor and contrary to pro-poor policies.

Box 9: For whom are cities built?

There is growing evidence that building codes, zoning regulations and public sector land management policies and procedures are biased against the urban poor. In a major research study – 'Regulatory Guidelines for Affordable Shelter' – sponsored by DFID, Payne concludes:

> This suggests that governance issues are central to the problem of access to legal shelter. The case studies reveal that it can require many steps to obtain planning permission to develop a residential plot and that this can take several years. To 'facilitate' a more rapid processing of applications usually requires a 'consideration' or payment to the officials on the basis that 'a favour granted requires a favour returned'… such payments can be seen as rampant corruption…
>
> (Payne 2003, p 3)

However, the problem is more pervasive than just cumbersome procedures and corruption. The basic standards that urban authorities try to impose do not match the needs of the urban poor and are too costly for low-income families. More than 15 years ago Hardoy and Satterthwaite (1989) observed that illegal settlements in and around cities can be viewed as the development of cities which are more appropriate to local culture, climate and conditions than the plans produced by the governments.

Or in the words of Payne:

> Perhaps the most pervasive [finding] is a tendency for all the key components of urban planning regulations and standards to be based on inherited or imported models. None can be said to be based on a detailed, objective or sensitive assessment of local needs and resources. This raises the central question of what purpose planning regulations and standards are intensded to serve. It is not clear that they are intended to protect the public interest or local environment or balance private and public costs and interests… The fact that they have survived decades since national independence suggests that they also serve the interests of present political and administrative elites.
>
> (Payne 2003, p 9)

HIV/AIDS

The HIV/AIDS pandemic is not only a serious health problem but a major obstacle for the development of poor countries; for some regions of Africa it is the most important.

In some countries rural HIV rates are approaching or surpassing those for urban areas. However, prevalence of the disease is generally still higher in urban areas and particularly in the large cities and among high-risk groups. Data from Kenya, Burundi and Zambia (2001–2003) show urban rates more than twice those of rural for people aged between 15 and 49. In urban areas of South Africa 17.5 per cent of the same age group had contracted the disease compared to 10.5 per cent of the rural population.

A recent analysis confirms that higher levels of urbanization tend to facilitate the spread of the disease.[18] However, in severely affected countries HIV/AIDS can slow down urbanization and urban growth. For parts of Africa this seems to be the case now.

There are two reasons why urbanization may be slowed by HIV/AIDS: the first is that the natural population growth will decrease more in urban than in rural areas (because of higher HIV/AIDS incidence), and the second is that migration patterns are changing. When town dwellers fall ill they often return to their rural family home – as may surviving family members after a death. Rural dwellers who might otherwise have moved to town stay in the village when they become ill or have to look after relatives.

Slum dwellers are vulnerable and prevention efforts cannot be separated from efforts to reduce poverty and improve the living conditions of the urban poor. Lack of a reliable water supply aggravates the situation; for those already infected, ample clean water is a prerequisite.

Young Mwoki is HIV positive. Diagnosis and treatment of children with HIV is hampered in developing countries by a lack of proper testing kits and medication, a situation that is worsening as the number of AIDS orphans increases, according to UNICEF.

© AFP PHOTO/TONY KARUMBA

Table 7. Prevalence of HIV in pregnant women

Country	City	Year	HIV prevalence (%)
Burundi	Bujumbura	1998	18.6
Lesotho	Maseru	2000	42.2
Malawi	Blantyre	2001	28.5
Namibia	Windhoek	1998	22.7
Rwanda	Kigali	1998–99	13.3
Zambia	Lusaka	1998	27.1
Zimbabwe	Harare	1999	31.1

Source: US Census bureau (2002) according to T Dyson HIV/AIDS and urbanization

18) Dyson, Tim (2003) 'HIV/AIDS and urbanization'. *Population and Development Review 29(3).*

The situation in the transition economies differs in many ways from that of the developing world. However, the urbanization process is surprisingly similar and such major problems as urban poverty and inequality, HIV/AIDS and poor governance are common to both.

Urban challenges in the transition countries

Urban situation

The transition economies in Eastern Europe and Central Asia have a legacy of central planning, state control of the economy and limited freedom for people to move. Still, the relationship between the level of economic development and urbanization is essentially identical to that for other developing countries (Figure 9). However, in most other respects, urban managers in transition economies face challenges quite different from those encountered by their peers in other parts of the developing world.

While most cities in the developing world struggle to accommodate rapidly growing urban populations, cities in the transition countries face a much less daunting task: because natural population growth is low, urban growth is generally below 1 per cent per annum and in some cases is even negative.

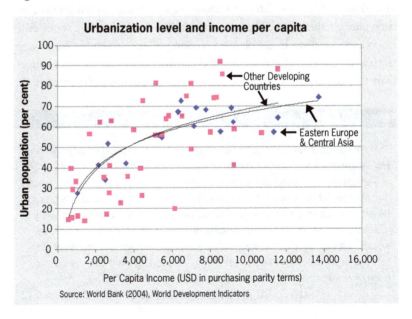

FIGURE 9.
Relationship between urbanization level and income per capita for transition economies and developing countries.

Cities in the transition economies differ also in other ways from most third world cities. Most people live in blocks of flats. There are few slum areas without infrastructure. Nearly all urban dwellers have electricity, and most have running water. In the Kyrgyz capital of Bishkek about 70 per cent of the population have household connections. The comparable figure for Lagos in Nigeria (a country with similar per capita income) is 6 per cent. However, slums are a problem in some countries. In FYR Macedonia, for example, 15–25 per cent of the urban population live in sub-standard, quasi-legal settlements.

The transition process has been accompanied by increased poverty and inequalities particularly in urban populations. Household poverty increased five times in Eastern Europe and Central Asia between 1990 and 2002. The serious social effects were an increase in alcoholism, suicide and mortality; declining or even negative population growth; and HIV/AIDS is spreading rapidly.

The most salient environmental concerns are serious pollution of air, water and soil in and around many cities. Ignorance and neglect during the old regime has left a heritage of contaminated soils, lakes and rivers and a stock of large industrial and power production plants lacking an efficient and effective technology to prevent emissions. Sewerage and industrial effluents are still often discharged with little or no treatment. Airborne emissions and pollution of rivers and coastal areas affect neighbouring countries.

Municipalities in transition

Traditionally, the state, through various organizations, owned housing estates, public transport and the infrastructure for district heating, water, sanitation and electricity. In the planned economy all investment decisions were taken at central or regional levels and financing came from the state budget. Only the day-to-day management of service provision was delegated to the

---

Box 10: The feminisation of poverty in Russia

The new economic situation has forced many women out of formal employment or into the informal job market, where social supports are negligible. A growing number of women-headed households are now deprived of the former state-provided services that were part of the safety net: child care, health care and other social supports. Recent research on female poverty in Russia suggests that feminisation of poverty manifests itself not only in the high probability of inclusion in the poor category by income, but that the female poverty shows exceptional patterns in the form of stagnant and extreme poverty (the poorest among the poor). Single-mother families and elderly women present the highest poverty risks.

UN-HABITAT The State of the World's Cities 2004/2005, box 5.12

---

local level but was still not a municipal task. With the fall of the Soviet Union the system collapsed. Operations continued at the local level, but maintenance and new investments were seriously neglected due to lack of resources, but also because the necessary legislative reforms took time.

Today service delivery is a municipal responsibility, but the accumulated need for repair and renewal of infrastructure systems is overwhelming, and the investments cannot be financed at the municipal level. The municipalities and their utilities may decide on tariffs, but major taxes are paid in to the region or the state, and transfers from higher levels of government are still needed. However, it is true that regional and local governments in Eastern Europe and Central Asia do collect about one-third of all taxes, which means they do have more funds to draw upon than most of their peers in other developing countries.

Housing and infrastructure

The housing stock was privatized to varying degrees during the 1990s but with little attention paid to the need for a supporting institutional framework. Although condominium associations and/or co-operatives of homeowners have been created, these have been slow to assume full responsibility for maintenance of the buildings and of common facilities. Rents in housing estates owned by the municipalities are generally too low to cover maintenance costs. The inevitable consequence is that the housing stock is decaying.

In the past, most new housing was financed by the state. Some public housing continues to be built for low-income households, but most construction and financing is now market based. However, in most of the transition countries, long-term mortgage financing hardly exist. The rate of new building is far below what it was before the reform process started.

A private rental market is slowly emerging – usually in the form of an apartment owner leasing a unit to tenants. Apartment blocks for rental are not being built. One reason is lack of long-term financing, but weak demand is also an important factor.

The systemic problems associated with the transition to a market economy are acute in district heating – typically provided by semi-autonomous municipal enterprises. Due to removal of the implicit energy subsidies, people in the transition economies may spend 5–10 per cent, the poor as much as 20 per cent of their income on heating (Lampietti & Meyer, 2003). It is universally acknowledged that most district heating systems are inefficient and lose a significant amount of energy. Improving efficiency in the generation and distribution of heat would help, but poorly insulated buildings and a lack of demand side management instruments are part of the problem. Reducing drafts through the windows, installing meters for

heat at the building level, and for domestic hot water at apartment level can be highly cost-effective and have pay-back periods of 1–2 years. In short, actions are required at the system, building and apartment levels.

However, the needed investments do not take place. Municipal enterprises and owners are unable to access long-term financing and households which do not pay per heating unit have no incentive to conserve energy.

Many Eastern European countries have commissioned the private sector to improve their water and sanitation systems, but the majority of the systems are operated – adequately – by municipalities. While technical and financial problems remain in water supply, the main investment needs are for sewage treatment.

The transition economies in Central Asia are, however, facing more serious problems. Consumer tariffs are inadequate to cover operation, maintenance and replacement investments and central government subsidies have been severely curtailed. Inadequate functioning of water treatment plants, badly deteriorated distribution networks and intermittent service have made drinking water unsafe in many urban centres, leading to a rise in water-borne diseases such as typhoid and diarrhoea.

In Baku (Azerbaijan), for example, 95 per cent of households are connected to the pipe system but they have water only for four hours per day five days a week. Not surprisingly, nine out of ten residents in the city regard the water as unsafe and virtually everybody boils it before drinking. Losses are also high and few customers have meters. In Bishkek (Kyrgyz Republic), for example, 30–40 per cent of the water is unaccounted for and only 1 per cent of domestic and 14 per cent of commercial customers are metered.

However, as illustrated by Yerevan (Armenia), progress is feasible: in 2004 half the population had 24-hour water while five years earlier the norm was six hours per day; more than 80 per cent of households are individually metered today compared to less than 0.5 per cent in 1999; collection performance over the same period went from 21 per cent to 100 per cent.

FURTHER READING
Hardoy, Jorge E. & David Satterthwaite (1989) *Squatter Citizen: Life in the Urban Third World*. Earthscan, London.
UN-HABITAT (2003) *The challenge of Slums – Global Report on Human Settlements 2003*. Earthscan, London.
UN-HABITAT (2003) *Water and Sanitation in the World´s Cities.Local action for global goals*. Earthscan, London.

4. MANAGING URBAN GROWTH

Poverty is not the only reason for slums and inadequate infrastructure – these are also the outward sign of failed policies, bad governance, inappropriate legal and regulatory frameworks, dysfunctional land markets, unresponsive financial systems, corruption and – last but not least – a lack of political will.

Critical issues

Managing the rapid urban growth in developing countries is a complex task. Sustainable urban development requires actions on many fronts. There is no one-stop solution.

However, it is possible to identify some critical issues and responses:

1. Improved urban governance and strengthened management capacity

2. Decentralization and devolution of powers and fiscal responsibilities from central government to local levels

3. Explicit pro-poor policies at local and national levels. Such policies must recognize the realities of the poor, their settlements and their occupation and must protect their rights.

4. Education and health services and protection against crime and violence equally available to all citizens.

5. Recognition of the urban poor, both women and men, as active agents of development rather than passive beneficiaries. Opportunities for participation must be broadened

6. Realistic planning ensuring, in particular, that land is made available for new housing in the growing cities.

7. Reduction of air and water pollution and development of recycling concepts to minimize the ecological footprint of urban centres.

8. Recognition that urban development has to rely primarily on domestic resources. Mobilisation of resources for local development both in the private and public sector (eg through improved municipal finances), is thus strategic. Sustainable financing of housing, infrastructure investments and service provision to be developed.

9. Making land and housing markets work, even for the poor.

Required actions include policy reforms at national level, improved legal systems and revised regulations, empowered local authorities and more appropriate financial markets. Communities, civil society and the private sector have to be involved.

Good urban governance is probably the most important factor of all. Broad and sustainable urban development depends on a political leadership that is committed to a democratic and equitable vision of urban society. Local authorities need strengthening and empowerment.

Governance

Empowerment of local authorities

In most poor countries central government retains responsibility for many tasks which in more developed countries are the responsibility of the local authority. The weak capacity at the municipal level is an explanation, but this weakness is also caused by central governments' reluctance to devolve power and failure to strengthen the local authorities.

Ultimately, development happens as a result of local efforts and local resources. These are mobilised only when the people themselves are involved, committed and feel 'ownership'. This means that management of resources and services needs to be as close as possible to the people for whom they are intended.

The only representative democratic governance structure at the local level is the elected assembly, the local council. NGOs, CBOs, stakeholder groups, civil society, business partnerships and ad hoc assemblies can all support, but lack the legitimacy of the democratically elected authority.

In some countries so-called decentralization policies during the last 15 years have transferred responsibility and resources to the local level, but the devolution of power has really only started. Figure 8 (p 68) shows that there is still a long way to go. Municipalities in developing countries are normally responsible for solid waste collection and often also urban roads. Half of them provide fire protection, primary education and health care, and only 20 per cent are responsible for water and sewerage. The decentralization process must be accelerated. Urban infrastructure, town planning and land management, environmental issues, slum upgrading and safety should normally all be a direct responsibility of the local government with support from central government. However, even the concept of 'decentralization' can be questioned. The assumption is that a range of local matters belongs to the central government but could be 'decentralized'. Perhaps the assumption should instead be that they are natural local concerns; they should perhaps never have been centralized in the first place, and that it is high time responsibility was reclaimed.

It is evident that a democratic local government with broader responsibilities must have the wherewithal to carry out the tasks. What is needed

Brazilian police patrol Rio de Janeiro's Rocinha slum. Police killed the head of a drug-trafficking gang who controlled Rio de Janeiro's biggest slum in a shoot-out a few days earlier. Erismar Rodrigues Moreira, known as Bem-Te-Vi, was the most wanted man in the crime-ridden city. He was said to be popular with some residents of Rocinha because he helped provide for their needs.

© REUTERS-Scanpix/
Bruno Domingos

Supported by Sweden, the Government of Botswana in 1988 commissioned a review and revision of its *Development Control Code*. This *code* regulates spatial development under the Town and Country Planning Act. The review showed that the code favoured those with higher incomes; those with low incomes on 'site-and-services' plots were deprived of livelihood opportunities like letting space and earning an income from working at home. The new code is fair to all. It allows even the poor to match the code stipulations, and even benefit from it. Serviced plots can be smaller, the space maximized, and the building flexible to allow work from home.

The code has been in operation since 1995. The verdict by an inclusive range of stakeholders is that it is clearly pro-poor and enabling. Devolved planning powers – inspired by the positive effects of the code – will give local authorities discretion in their application of the code. They can decide case-by-case. Planning prerequisites then, will enable and encourage rather than constrain. The informal economy – particularly important to women – is finally recognized; letting and no-nuisance informal economic activities' are now legal.

Nils Viking, PhD, Royal Institute of Technology, Stockholm,
Architect and Planner, who participated in the preparation of the new code

is a fiscal reform which will increase local taxation making local authorities less dependent on unreliable, irregular and insufficient transfers from the national budget (see 'Poor municipalities', p 67).

Even the future role of the municipality needs to be reconsidered. Given the challenges to manage urban growth and combat poverty, it is not enough to see the municipality simply as a traditional provider of essential services. A more pro-active role and a broader responsibility for local development will be required. The South African constitution, which has assigned this task to the local government, could serve as an example.

Any reform to empower local authorities will have to be adapted according to their size, and to the situation in the country. Reform needs to be accompanied by systematic strengthening of their institutional capacity. The associations of local governments could play a role together with the ministry in charge.

The key role of the central government

Failed policies and inappropriate legal and regulatory frameworks are fundamental obstacles to sustainable, pro-poor, urban development.

Beside the reforms required to devolve power and fiscal authority to local authorities as described above, the central government needs to revise or develop new policies and intervene in several critical areas:

Governance
- establish an adequate governance structure at ministerial level for urban development;
- establish effective policies and institutions to prevent corruption and with independent control systems at all levels;
- enhance the capacity of local governments and other actors through training, institutional support, research and higher education;
- develop environmental regulations that prevent urban centres from placing excessive environmental burdens onto the surrounding regions.

Policy reform
- incorporate urban poverty in Poverty Reduction Strategies recognising its particularities and special needs;
- develop a comprehensive housing policy including, where feasible, a financially sustainable system of subsidies targeting the poor and prioritising basic infrastructure;
- revise obsolete and unaffordable building codes and regulations and enact a realistic and enforceable legislative framework that reflects the needs of the urban poor in particular with respect to plot size, incremental construction, affordable building materials and home-based economic activities;
- undertake reform of public utilities, ensuring commercialisation and privatization (when appropriate) and establish the regulatory framework.

Security, equal rights
- enact legislation against forced evictions and provide security of tenure with particular attention to the equal rights of women to own and inherit land and other property;
- strengthen protection and prevention of crime and violence with special regard to the most affected through legislation, enforcement and through community-based prevention programmes;
- ensure that education, health services and HIV/AIDS programmes reach the poor urban dwellers, even in informal and unauthorized settlements.

Economy, finance
- revise legislation and policies in order to facilitate integration of the informal economy into the formal system;
- plan and secure long term availability of water and electricity;
- promote the development of functioning housing finance services including savings and micro-finance institutions serving the poor;
- facilitate more effective land and housing markets and the supply of land for future urban growth;
- finance nation-wide initiatives and major infrastructure investments from the national budget and through loans from IFIs.

Civil society participation is essential

Active civil society organizations are an important complement to, or even a prerequisite of, good governance.

Numerous non-governmental organizations carry out invaluable work to improve the conditions of the poor, but they also have an important advocacy role in the public debate and as governance 'watch-dogs'.

In Bangalore, India and in Curitiba, Brazil, the watch-dog role for monitoring municipal service delivery has even been institutionalized.

Ideally, collaboration between the local authority and the civil society should be beneficial. Unfortunately, government may not see the benefit; they fear opposition and will not invite or welcome close scrutiny.

Since NGOs often act as advocates for the poor, they are sometimes perceived as representing the poor. And sometimes NGOs act as if they had this mandate – a serious mistake. The poor have the right to speak and act for themselves. The relationships are clear as long as the urban poor are seen as active agents rather than passive recipients. When improvement plans are discussed and decided the perspective and priorities of the poor themselves should apply.

One of the most promising recent approaches to involve the poor and to create real ownership and substantive participation has been through negotiated agreements. Local governments and slum dwellers have agreed to work together on concrete projects where both parties contribute. Here the poor put forward their views, these are taken seriously, and a deal is negotiated and agreed.

In this context NGOs can play an important role in helping the poor to form democratic organizations such as slum federations and other CBOs, which could represent them. The NGOs can then argue that the local government must acknowledge and consult these organizations and help bringing the two parties together.

Human rights

If human rights on equal terms were adopted as the principle for governance, the prevailing conditions of the urban poor would not exist. It is not poverty as such, nor is it only the lack of public resources that produces urban misery, but also unequal power structures and irresponsible political leadership.

Human rights, rule of law and gender equality are very relevant issues in relation to urban poverty. Fundamentally, it is a matter of human equality, and the rights of the poor and vulnerable are always at risk in the extremely un-

Sammy Gitau walks on a street in one of Nairobi's slums. A former street boy, Gitau now leads a project which tries to give children some basic education, training and sports activities. His Mathare Community Resource Centre is one of many African-run grassroots organizations struggling to make life better for the urban poor.

© REUTERS/Scanpix

Antony Njuguna

Table 8. Urban poor/homeless federations and their supporters

Examples of urban poor/homeless federations, their support NGOs and the funds that support their work. There are also federations developing in Malawi, Swaziland, Nepal and Zambia, and savings groups that have the potential to form federations are being set up in many other nations, including Uganda, Ghana, Lesotho, Tanzania and Madagascar.

Federation	Year founded	Number of members	Support /NGO federation-managed funds
INDIA: National Slum Dwellers Federation and *Mahila Milan*	1974 and 1986	ca. 2 million plus	SPARC (1984) Community-Led Infrastructure Finance Facility (CLIFF)
SOUTH AFRICA: *uMfelanda Wonye* (South African Homeless People's Federation)	1991	ca. 100,000	People's Dialogue on Land and Shelter The *uTshani* Fund (for housing), *Inqolobane* (The Granary) funds for employment/microenterprise
ZIMBABWE: The Zimbabwe Homeless People's Federation	1993	ca. 45,000	Dialogue on Shelter *Gungano* Fund
NAMIBIA: Shack Dwellers Federation of Namibia	1992	9,700	Namibian Housing Action Group (1997)
KENYA: *Muungano wa Wanvijiji*	2000	ca. 25,000	Pamoja Trust (2000) *Akiba Mashinani*
THAILAND: Various regional and city-based federations	1990	Thousands of savings groups	CODI – fund set up by the government of Thailand
PHILIPPINES: Philippines Homeless People's Federation	2003	50,000	Vincentian Missionaries Social Development Foundation Inc (VMSDFI) Urban Poor Development Fund
SRI LANKA: Women's Development Bank	1998	31,000	JANARULAKA Women's Development Bank Federation
CAMBODIA: Squatter and Urban Poor Federation	1994	Active in 200 slums	Asian Coalition for Housing Rights Urban Poor Development Fund

D'Cruz, Celine and Satterthwaite (2005) *Building Homes, Changing Official Approaches: The Work of Urban Poor Organizations and their Federations and their Contributions to Meeting the Millennium Development Goals in Urban Areas* IIED, London

In Mumbai, the Indian Railways needed to clear thousands of households off land immediately adjacent to the railway tracks, because this was hölding down the speed of trains. Discussions with the Railway Slum Dwellers Federation showed that most wanted to move, if they could get a home with secure tenure not too far from their sources of income. A relocation programme was developed through negotiations between this federation and government agencies, supported by a local NGO (SPARC). All those who were to be resettled were involved in the timing and organization of the move, the choice of location to which they moved and the management of the relocation sites. Some 60 000 people were relocated with no violence and no need for police to enforce this.

Agreements between city governments in Pune and Mumbai and slum dwellers' organizations (including *Mahila Milan* – savings groups formed by women) has also led to hundreds of community-designed, built and managed toilet blocks with washing facilities in the slums. They are of better quality and better managed than government-constructed toilets and cost no more.

Environment and Urbanization Vol. 14, No. 1 and Vol.15, No. 2

equal urban society. Here the poorest of the poor live just over the garden wall from the richest of the rich The rich see beggars, street vendors and squatters as a nuisance and a potential threat. They have economic and political power and public resources tend to be used to satisfy their needs even when the official line is that the service is to benefit the poor. Subsidized water tariffs benefit those with piped water, subsidized public housing is often occupied by the middle class. Poor settlements would benefit from safe paths or access roads, but the money is instead spent on roundabouts and highways.

Since the poor often live in separate communities, there is a spatial dimension to discrimination. Areas with a poor population tend to be neglected in terms of infrastructure, basic services, education and health facilities. The poor of course also settle where the land costs are affordable, which usually means that infrastructure and services are not available. The result is the exclusion and segregation found in cities all over the world.

In order to protect their rights and have their voice heard, the poor need to form democratic organizations. Established power structures in unequal societies, however, tend to fear these organizations: the poor are frustrated, and the young poor especially can become politically volatile and destabilising.

One of the most pertinent rights issue in an urban context is the lack of secure tenure. Many poor households still face the risk of forceful eviction, which usually takes place without notice (in order to avoid organized resistance). The events in Zimbabwe in 2005, when the homes of 700 000 poor were bulldozed, is a sad example of political repression, but was defended by the Government with the argument that the intention was to 'clean up and beautify the city' – as if that would justify the violation (see Box 3, p 33).

Human rights have to be protected by law, but that is not enough. The rights must also be known and culturally adopted. This will require education, information, advocacy – and time. Equal rights for women to own and inherit land and property are – as mentioned before – legally protected in many countries, but often not respected because old traditions are stronger.

New or improved legislation is needed to enhance the protection of human rights, particularly with respect to the poor and vulnerable. The civil society has an advocacy role in this context.

Accountability and transparency

Governments in developing countries could do more to create trust in their policies. Trust is fundamental for mobilising those human and financial resources, which are a prerequisite for development.

The local authorities deal with matters belonging to everyday life. When there are deficiencies and failures, these will be experienced by everyone. If properly informed, people may understand and accept such shortcomings, but they will lose confidence in government if they do not understand why things do not work, and if they do not believe that the government is making reasonable efforts to improve the situation.

Development requires, as already stressed, contributions from all sectors of society. The local government has an important role, but if people lack confidence in the government, then local resources will not be mobilised and development will be hampered. With broader responsibilities and extended taxation authority the need for transparency and accountability will become even greater.

There are several risk factors at the local governance level. The political power may be concentrated in one person – the mayor – and without real checks and balances. Increased local self-governance would require not only strengthening of the institutional capacity and technical support, but also better information for the citizens, professional audits and a national system for monitoring of municipal performance. There is a need to develop a democratic culture at local level. 'Clientalism' and the appointment of political cronies to municipal jobs after each election cannot continue if local authorities should take their obligations to the citizens seriously.

The new generation in Phnom Penh, Cambodia. The upper and middle classes in many urban centres are growing rapidly and adopting new consumer habits. This is particularly evident in the booming Asian economies.

© Jean-Léo Dugast / PHOENIX

Transparency is also required at the project level – for instance when the municipality, or other authority is to implement projects which affect the local community. If a project is based on participation from the community, eg through a negotiated agreement as described above, it is of vital importance that all information is freely available, especially on the project finances and how the parties are to fulfil their respective obligations. Participation and ownership will not develop if the poor are patronised. This also applies to projects implemented by NGOs. The Prodel programme (Box 4, p 41) is an example of a 'joint venture' between municipalities and communities for local infrastructure works. Here confidence between the parties was created in spite of the deep initial distrust after a civil war. This was possible thanks to clear game rules, transparency and accountability from the municipalities at project level.

Corruption

'Corruption is the antithesis of good governance: inherently covert rather than open and transparent; exclusive rather than inclusive and communicative; divisive rather than coherent and integrative; immoral rather than equitable and ethical.'[19]

Corruption is when people violate their duties for personal or political gain. When this behaviour is widespread, it is like an infectious disease hard to cure, in particular where it is an endemic feature of the culture. It undermines good governance and the perverse effect on resource allocation is detrimental to all development efforts – a veritable 'killing factor'. Corruption is often seen as a public sector evil. This is a mistake. Corrupt behaviours in the private sector are no less damaging. Corruption in different sectors and levels tend to reinforce each other. It is, indeed, corrupt 'public-private partnerships', which are most serious and which involve huge amounts.

Combating corruption is difficult and needs a wide range of actions at all levels. The risk for large-scale corruption is most evident at the national level since it is the central government which controls most of the financial resources and is responsible for major investments. This puts a limit to the scale of corruption at the level of the local government except in major cities. The risks will increase, however, if the municipalities are granted a broader mandate and more resources in the future. Preventive countermeasures must certainly be in place.

In the urban context there are numerous opportunities for small-scale corruption, adding costs to many transactions. This is a nuisance for every-

---

19) McGranahan, Gordon and Satterthwaite, David (2004) *Governance and Getting the Private Sector to Provide better Water and Sanitation Services to the Urban Poor*, Thematic Paper for UN-HABITAT Urban Forum in Barcelona 2004.

one and not least for the poor. Local regulations require many types of permits. Often there is a fee to be paid to the municipality, but the applicant may also have to pay a bribe to get the permit or for faster processing.

Another similar form of corruption is when local businessmen pay for favourable treatment in relation to land allocation, location of industrial or commercial investments, exceptions from environmental requirements, special consideration in contract allocation and so forth.

The water and sanitation sector provides examples of various forms of corruption. They range from corrupt relations between utilities and their customers and corrupt relations between utilities and their contractors. In a recent study in nine locations in South Asia, 41 per cent of the 411 customers interviewed admitted that they had paid for false meter readings, 30 per cent had paid to expedite repair works and 12 per cent had paid to get a new connection.[20] In at least one location customers made payments to a line worker to avoid being reported for illegal connections. The amounts involved were usually small and the practice is very much a consequence of ineffective water management. If an operator curbs this type of corruption the effect on low-income customers could in fact be negative if the regular service provision did not improve. So poor neighbourhoods already suffering from poor service and corruption could also suffer from efforts to curb corruption.

The same study found frequent corruption in contracting procedures: funds for construction were 'skimmed' and shared by a number of different actors. Findings indicated kickbacks in the range of 5-10 per cent of contract value in every second contract. These extra costs are passed on to the consumers.

According to the Asian study, successful anti-corruption strategies included increased accountability and increased cost of misconduct (or benefits from good conduct). In low-income areas the involvement of the residents themselves in quality control seems to be most successful – like the system of 'scorecards' in Bangalore (p 88). The fight against corruption is difficult and even more so if both the police and the legal system are corrupt. Unfortunately, this is not rare. The urban poor generally do not expect any help or protection from the police – on the contrary – in many places they are harassed by the police and often forced to pay bribes or 'fines', without cause.

Both efficient control systems and a culture of democracy, transparency and accountability are required to prevent corruption. Education, well-designed incentives and consistent leadership could contribute to shape an anti-corrupt corporate culture in public administration. In countries where corruption is the norm as for example in parts of Asia it will take a long time to change value systems and behaviour.

---

20) Davis, J (2004) 'Corruption in public water supply; Experiences from South Asia's water and sanitation sector', *World Development, Elsevier,* vol 32 no 1

Urban development planning must involve all stakeholders and be comp-
rehensive and holistic. One of the biggest challenges is to provide land for
the growing population and to promote local economic development.
Urban transport and management of the environment are other key areas.

Urban management

Inclusive city development strategies

Urban development is a complex process. It involves housing and technical systems for water supply, sanitation and storm water drainage, energy, tele-communications and transports – all with high investment costs. Schools, clinics and other social services have to be developed, parks and recreation areas must be provided. Building regulations to guarantee public safety, hygiene and environmental protection have to be established and enforced and all development must take future expansion into account.

Many, often conflicting, interests are involved. Private and public inter-est, environmental concerns, the protection of cultural heritage and other aspect should all be considered. The economic consequences of infrastruc-ture investments and other development initiatives are considerable since they create business opportunities, raise the cost of land and have an impact on rents and property values.

There are many stakeholders and some are more powerful than others. The majority of the population, the urban poor, are not powerful at all. They, as well as other interested parties, may easily be excluded from plan-ning and decision procedures.

Urban development is therefore a difficult political and technical issue, which requires democratic governance and management guided by profes-sionalism and a vision of social, economical and environmental sustainabili-ty. In reality, the planning capacity of most local authorities in developing countries is very limited. Unfortunately, it is also fragmented. One na-tional authority may be responsible for water and another for power supply while a third agency may have charge of the distribution grid; the munici-pality may be responsible for sewerage and local roads while the national road authority is responsible for major roads – and so forth.

New methods have been developed to involve all stakeholders in dev-elopment planning and to facilitate coordination. Like the city-wide con-sultations introduced through Urban Management Programme (UMP) and the city development strategies promoted by Cities Alliance (Box 13), these are a means to form a more inclusive process and to reach a compact on

As defined by Cities Alliance: "The city development strategy (CDS) is a process by which elected representatives together with local stakeholders define their vision for the city and its economic growth, environmental and poverty reduction objectives, with clear priorities for actions and investments."

A CDS is an action plan for equitable growth in cities, developed and sustained through participation, to improve the quality of the life for all citizens. The goals of a CDS include a collective city vision and action plan aimed at improving urban governance and management, increasing investment to expand employment and services, and systematic and sustained reduction in urban poverty.

An initial analysis/assessment of development challenges (baseline data, socio-economic maps etc), provides decision-makers with substantive information about the city and its region, needed as a basis for monitoring and evaluation and for analysing future trends, challenges and opportunities.

essential development issues for the city.[21] An important advantage is that since different groups and stakeholders are able to argue for their concerns and priorities, decisions will be well-informed. As always, there is a risk that the poor, if not properly organized, are left out of the process.

The consultative and inclusive planning methods are an important complement rather than a substitute for more conventional spatial urban planning; this is still required. Physical planning is a double-edged instrument. It is indispensable for coordinated development, but obsolete or unrealistic plans always create problems. However, the rapidly growing population, the expansion of infrastructure systems and the protection of the environment certainly do need professional physical planning.

Land management

There is no lack of land. The problem is dysfunctional land markets, misguided regulations and a lack of pro-active land management policies.

One of the most critical issues for the poor in growing urban centres is lack of affordable land for housing. More effective land and housing markets would improve the situation and remove one of the obstacles for economic development as well. Legislative reforms and revised regulations allowing

---

21) Global programme initiated by UNDP, WB and UN-HABITAT in 1986. Managed by UN-HABITAT and supported by several bilateral donors (including Sweden) during almost twenty years, UMP has contributed to develop and transfer know-how on urban management issues. UMP has also developed institutional capacity in all regions to provide advisory services at city level.

small plots, mixed land use, incremental housing and affordable infrastructure are required.

This is not enough, though, and local authorities have to face the land issue in a pro-active manner. In some countries and cities, considerable land resources are publicly owned and local authorities can allocate land for low-income housing. The poor are rarely able to pay the full commercial price. Plots and basic services may be partly subsidized and lease arrangements could allow cost coverage over time.

If public land is not available for current and future needs, the local authority should acquire reserves of land for urban expansion. Well managed, this would allow the municipality to sell some plots at market price to other developers. The increase in land value thanks to urban expansion could cover at least part of the subsidy to the poor. In poor countries with weak municipalities the financing of land purchases would need support from the central government.

Another option for local authorities is to negotiate building rights with private landowners on condition that parcels of land are reserved for the poor. A variety of this is practised in Brazil, where all landowners are given a certain building right and are allowed to buy additional rights – with the proceeds used in the public interest. Sao Paulo has even issued 'rights bonds' on the market.

Providing security of tenure

Security of tenure is a fundamental requirement. If you always have the fear of eviction hanging over you, then you have little incentive to invest hard work or hard-earned money into your house or workshop.

It is often assumed that secure tenure would require formal property titles. Formal individual titling, however, is a costly procedure which requires surveying and registration. Large-scale legal tenure reforms are practically impossible due to the very limited capacity of developing country cadastral services.

Other tenure forms can satisfy the most important needs of the poor. These needs are: not to be evicted, to have access to basic services, to be able to sell or transfer their plot and house. These needs can all be met without formal titles. It is only for mortgage loans that these are essential, and conventional mortgages are anyway not suited to the poor (see 'Only bankers can get mortgages', p 58).

Most experts now advocate an approach to tenure that includes announcing a stop to forced evictions and relocations, and promoting records of land use and occupancy rights with an incremental upgrading of rights over time (eg Cities Alliance, 2002; and UN-HABITAT, 2003, p. 171). The provision of basic services, street numbering, voter rolls and of identity cards are examples of implicit recognition of a settlement that provide a simple and affordable security of tenure.

Lusaka City Council issues 30-year (renewable) occupancy licenses to informal settlement dwellers. This might explain why most houses are built with permanent materials.

With political will, it is also possible to simplify and streamline bureaucratic procedures.[22] In the 1990s, the procedure for land titling and registering property in Peru was simplified, the cost reduced to USD 50 and the time required cut to six weeks or less. In five years, more than a million households were given titles to their properties (Panaritis 2001).

Urban transport – more harm than good for the poor?

The rapid increase in the use of private cars and motorbikes is a major threat to urban centres all over the world. Congestion, traffic accidents, pollution and emission of greenhouse gases are serious problems.

The economic advantage of urban centres depends on communication. Poor transport networks reduce the agglomeration economies and are a major constraint for economic growth in bigger cities. Hence, a major challenge of urban planning is to establish a spatial structure with an effective system for road transport, which is the principal mode for transport of goods and people in urban centres, although other systems also exist, which we discuss later. The planning decisions and the investments in the road network are extremely important since they will direct the development of a city for generations to come. The network of roads and streets tends to remain as long as the town exists — much longer than buildings.

Different urban planning patterns generate different transport needs. Extended, low density urban concepts as in North America, South Africa and parts of Latin America require individual transport and promote the use of private cars. 'Urban sprawl', meaning the trend to chose peripheral locations where land is cheap for commerce and offices, also depends on private car ownership and increases traffic volumes. By contrast, the traditional 'European' town-planning model favours more concentrated settlement patterns and a development coordinated with the layout of public transport systems. Hence the need to use private vehicles is reduced.

---

22) Nordin, Benita and Östberg, Tommy (2000) *Urban Growth and Cadastral Development – a manual for the development of appropriate cadastral methods for cities and towns in developing countries,* Swedesurvey and Sida, Gävle and Stockholm

Curitiba started to develop an organized public transport system based on buses on dedicated bus-ways in the 1970s, when the city found that it could not afford an urban rail system. In existing central areas, part of the road and street capacity was redistributed from cars to buses, while in new areas separate bus-ways were built from the beginning.

Buses in Curitiba move people from place to place as quickly as the New York subways, but at a fraction of the cost. The network is centrally organized and planned as one coherent and integrated system – not as a series of competing routes. There are express routes and nodes for changing to trunk routes and distribution routes. In the famous tube stations, passengers have already paid for the trip and board the bus very rapidly. Route packages are operated by private bus companies and the whole system runs without subsidies.

Urban transport systems are a common good requiring long-term planning and huge investments. Most of the benefits are usually yielded in the future, when current political mandates have expired. Political vision and consistency is thus required. This is what explains the success of transport planning in Curitiba, Brazil – probably the most well known 'best practice' in urban transport. The objectives were defined early and then pursued over a long period of time thanks to continuity of the political leadership. Changes in political power otherwise often mean a break with previous policies, which is unfortunate in areas where continuity is extremely important.

Urban transport is also an area with frequent conflicts of interests. Here pro-poor policies are badly needed to protect the interests of the poor and ensure that investments also benefit them. Transportation is a fundamental need for poor residents in peri-urban areas, but it is also a major source of problems, and investments in urban transport infrastructure often constitute a substantial drain on the municipal budget. The traffic problems, the lack of transportation facilities and the costs for poor households are major concerns. A low-income urban family in Africa may spend one-third of its earnings on transport.

The most pressing problem for many local authorities in growing urban centres is the increase of motorised traffic causing congestion, accidents and air pollution. Investing in urban transport is often equated with providing more space for cars. This is rarely of any advantage to the poor. In fact, road construction is the leading cause for forced evictions and resettlement, and new roads often slice through a neighbourhood, making it hard for people to go about their ordinary business.

Increased traffic also means more accidents – especially for the poor who normally walk or bike on poorly lit roads without sidewalks. More than 1.2

A bus rapid transit system (or metro bus system) such as here in Bogotá, is a cheap and effective solution for cities with transport problems. The buses have their own dedicated lanes, and move as quickly from place to place as subway trains. Studies have shown that a bus rapid transit system is also profitable for bus owners to operate and relatively inexpensive for commuters to use.

© Karl Fjellström

million people are killed in traffic accidents every year (Hook and Howe 2004) and two-thirds of accidents occur in developing countries. Besides the human suffering, traffic accidents represent economic losses to these countries equal to the entire amount of international aid, according to the 1998 *World Disaster Report* by the Red Cross/Red Crescent.

Land use planning and transport planning with particular emphasis on public transport, non-motorised transport, traffic safety and environmental control – would benefit not only the poor, but everyone in the city.

Growing urban centres need new roads, but road construction is expensive. Other solutions to improve the traffic situation are available at lower cost. The capacity of the existing system can be enhanced by improvements focusing on bottlenecks, efficient traffic management and better road maintenance. The utilization of private cars can be counteracted by regulation and by introducing economic disincentives like congestion charges and other fiscal measures. While alternative means of transportation also need to be promoted – for instance, through bus lanes, bicycle lanes and safe sidewalks and footpaths – in most developing country cities the need for improved road networks is indisputable.

Only small towns can function without any form of collective transport. In all other cases an affordable and reliable public transportation system is essential. A bus-based mass transit system is the most cost-efficient option as demonstrated in cities like Curitiba, Bogotá, Singapore and others.[23] Underground metro or light rail systems are much more expensive. These can only be justified in high-density cities, but in low-income countries they often become a permanent financial burden, while only solving part of the problem and rarely matching the needs of the poor. In Peru, the authorities could even not afford the running costs of a metro system financed by a European donor.

Urban transport policies need to shift focus from space for the movement of vehicles to access and safe mobility of people.

Managing the urban environment

Successful management of the urban environment is crucial for the future of the planet, but the global perspective should not overshadow the fact that the local environmental impact on poor peoples' health is an even worse immediate concern.

The environmental challenges were described previously (p 62). Many factors contribute to the unsustainable environmental situation of urban centres in the developing countries. Actions are needed in all areas and invol-

---

23) Singapore also has a very advanced rail system.

ve the society as a whole. Households, industry and the private and public sectors should all contribute. Adequate legislation is in place in many countries, but the enforcement and monitoring is often weak and needs strengthening at the local level. Better urban environmental management is a solution not only to local environmental problems but also to global problems.

In a situation of rapid urban growth, insufficient resources to expand and maintain infrastructure and urban services lead to serious environmental problems. These affect human health and the health of the poor in particular. A high concentration of people combined with an inadequate water supply and very poor sanitary conditions is the cause of disease and even death for millions of urban dwellers – mostly children. Improvement of sanitary conditions is therefore a most important environmental issue – especially for the urban poor. Where municipal services are lacking, it is all the more important that people are at least aware of environmental hazards, have the opportunity to take protective measures and as far as they are able, practice good hygiene. Hygiene education is a key issue – as important as improved services – since appropriate behaviour can reduce risks.

Waterborne sewerage systems with no (or malfunctioning) treatment plants cause pollution of rivers, lakes and coastal areas. The use of scarce water for sanitation and the loss of important nutrients – phosphorus in particular – are other concerns. The use of water-saving flush toilets and the construction of sewage treatment plants, which efficiently treat wastewater for re-use and transform sludge into a soil supplement are then seen as a solution. However, the sewage is often contaminated by chemicals and heavy metals that are difficult to remove. These prevent the use of the sludge as fertiliser.[24] The investment costs of a complete waterborne system with adequate sewage treatment even without the reuse of sludge is very high and in reality unaffordable for most urban centres in poor countries. Decentralized waterborne sewerage systems with only household connections (thus avoiding most of the chemical contamination) and local treatment can be an alternative or a complement. Ecological sanitation (Box 15) is very adequate in small towns and peri-urban areas together with urban agriculture.

Indoor air pollution remains a problem in urban areas, particularly where cooking and heating are done indoors with smoky fuels. Ambient air pollution caused by emissions from energy plants, industry, and traffic is increasing. Technical solutions to reduce harmful emissions are available though, and the situation in developed countries has improved. This will probably

---

24) Stockholm, Sweden, is an example. In spite of a very sophisticated sewage treatment system, the difficulties of satisfactorily removing heavy metals and some other substances have forced farmers to discontinue the use of sludge as a fertiliser.

FOOD

URINE
FAECES

PEOPLE

SOIL

CROPS

SAFE
FERTILIZER

Closing the loop

Ecological sanitation means sanitation that saves water, does not pollute and returns the nutrients in human excreta to the soil. Sweden has, through Sida, supported research and development in ecological sanitation for more than ten years and an international group of experts developed this alternative to the inadequate sanitation practises promoted today. It is a response to the challenges of the growing number of people without sanitation, the health effects of poor sanitation, the water shortage in many areas, the water pollution from current systems and the unsustainable flow of plant nutrients.

The basic features of ecological sanitation are simple. It is a matter of separating urine from faeces and making sure that contamination from faeces is prevented and disease organisms are effectively eliminated before re-use of the excreta product in agriculture. This can be achieved in several ways and there is a range of technical solutions from sophisticated systems for multi-story apartment buildings and dense urban areas to simple models for a single household in peri-urban areas (see also SEI 2004, *Ecological sanitation*).

A most important finding is that urine contains very few disease-producing organisms and is at the same time a valuable nutrient. Urine separation and its reuse in agriculture is both easy to manage and valuable from an ecological perspective.

Ecological sanitation is not novel – similar systems have been used for hundreds of years in different cultures and are still abundant in parts of Asia. In Western countries this option was largely abandoned when the waterborne systems were introduced. Now there is a revival of interest in ecological approaches to sanitation also in developed countries.

Successful examples of new systems are found particularly in Central America, China, Mexico, India, Sweden and Germany. In spite of low costs and environmental benefits ecological sanitation is still not well known. There are cultural barriers and established practises to overcome and it is not the solution for everywhere. In many urban centres of developing countries it should be an attractive option, however, and it is particularly indispensable in places where rocky ground conditions make other solutions impossible.

also happen in developing countries. Monitoring of air pollution, an important tool, could be used to identify critical areas and sources of pollution and to direct interventions. A global concern is the emission of carbon dioxide, the major greenhouse gas, and the contribution from developing countries is increasing.

The municipality is usually responsible for solid waste collection and management, but in most developing countries the service is poor. Garbage accumulates or is burned where people live – an environmental hazard. In informal settlements waste is rarely collected at all and it would certainly be difficult for the municipality to achieve cost recovery.

Industrial waste, hazardous waste and household waste present distinct problems. A comprehensive policy is required for the collection and treatment of all types of waste. The policy should in the first place aim at reducing the amounts of waste at source, particularly in more affluent neighbourhoods and in commercial and industrial areas. In the second place, waste should as far as possible be recycled and reused.

In developing countries the collected solid waste is usually dumped, and when the city grows the dump becomes a nuisance and a new site is needed. Finding a new location is often a problem, but relocation does provide the opportunity to use improved technology (sanitary landfill) and collect leachate which otherwise would contaminate streams and groundwater.

Waste handling is an important source of income for very poor people, both in the informal economy, but also as employed waste collection workers. When reorganising waste collection, the focus is often on acquiring new and sophisticated equipment. But large trucks are not appropriate for narrow streets in low-income areas, where a waste collection system rather could be based on human resources, community participation and more modest equipment. The Zabaleen waste collection and re-use in Cairo, Egypt, is an example of urban poor recycling waste. Since the Zabaleens are Coptic Christians, and thus allowed to eat pork, they feed pigs with the organic waste.

An underestimated problem is the lack of awareness of the environment and pollution within the informal economy; this results in pollution and occupational hazards. Information and advice is required.

Information is, in fact, needed in all areas of environmental management. Campaigns targeted at selected groups, including schools, is probably the most cost-efficient intervention that a local authority could undertake.

The spatial dimension of environmental management is often forgotten. Attention has been focused on legislation and regulation, Environmental Impact Assessments (EIAs) and permits, limits and so forth. In the urban context the spatial dimension is important and the location of industrial plants, sewage plants, fresh water production and water reserves, waste dumps, roads and the preservation of green areas are examples of land use decisions with important environmental consequences. Physical planning is therefore indispensable.

Cultural heritage and the historic environment

The cultural impact of urban societies is crucial for development and cultural heritage is an invaluable asset to all communities.

Our history survives in everything that we create, in buildings, in cultivated landscapes, in language, traditions and fairy-tales; it is all these creations that are our cultural heritage.

All urban centres have a physical heritage from the past, usually buildings or other structures or even entire urban areas. Some towns and cities in developing countries are very old and some are also included in UNESCO's *World Heritage List*. The historic environment is an asset and a resource. Its conservation and sustainable use may contribute to economic development and poverty reduction. (See Sida, 2005, *Urban Assets* and *Caring for the Historic Environment*)

Tourism is growing rapidly and historic cities and spectacular sites are obviously magnets that attract capital and business. In many places cultural heritage is the most important single asset, although its potential may not have been realized.

Yet the value of the historic environment cannot be measured in terms of potential economic benefits from tourism only. A nation or a people is held together by shared interests and memories – almost always associated with places. It is difficult to imagine memories of events, which are not localized in space. Hence, the urban (and rural) and architectural heritage has an important role as visible support to the collective memory of the past.

However, there are always painful events and periods of history, which the current generation might prefer to forget. Monuments or buildings representing colonialism, apartheid, 'other' religions or previous periods of social inequality may be uncomfortable reminders of repression, violence and old power structures. The wish to manifest the end of such periods – or simply the lack of consideration for this heritage – often leads to their destruction or deterioration in spite of their historical and cultural significance. This is understandable, and the argument here is not that everything should always be conserved. But art, architecture and cultural heritage possess their own values and it is, at any rate, futile to try to erase history. Therefore it is an important, but difficult, challenge for every society to liberate its historic environment from narrow ideological or ethnical identifications and to stop

Antanarivo, Madagascar. Some towns in developing countries are very old, and some are included in UNESCO's World Heritage List. Since the historic environment is an asset, its conservation and sustainable use may contribute to economic development and poverty reduction.

© Thomas Melin

Small-scale tourism-based enterprises advertising their services in Zanzibar stone town. Tourism may generate income for the local community, but spectacular sites may be taken over by big business and massive tourism could even be detrimental, if not developed with respect for the local environment.

© Thomas Melin

sacrificing valuable buildings and monuments for such reasons.

It is better to learn from history than to take revenge on it!

Management of the historic environment should be based on traditional crafts, methods and local materials. These are labour intensive and create jobs for local workers and contractors.

Historical cities and older parts of towns are often dilapidated and occupied by the poor. Restoration then necessarily affects the poor living or working there. Comprehensive restoration might result in gentrification – that the rents go up so that only the well-off can afford to live there. But in many cases it is possible and preferable to undertake only minor repairs to prevent further deterioration. If rehabilitation is planned and executed with participation from the inhabitants it can be adapted to their needs and affordable for many of them. When they can stay on in their homes and carry on with their business much of the life and character of the area can be preserved. Heritage is not only a matter of buildings – and a restoration that eliminates all original life, small shops and services from the area is a failure.

Empowerment of local authorities is not possible without fiscal reforms and local development is not possible without mobilisation of local resources.

Improving municipal finances

Transfers and taxes

Strengthening the ability of municipalities to effectively deliver services to their inhabitants requires actions on many different levels. The fiscal system needs to be reformed in most developing countries, increasing the local governments' taxing authority. Transfers to municipalities should be made automatic, predictable and transparent. The amount should be linked to some easily established criteria such as population, number of school children, etc. Municipalities should generally be given greater fiscal autonomy and be free to determine their expenditures without central government approval (subject, of course, to proper audits).

The access to infrastructure and the quality of services has a major influence on rents and property values. In Nairobi, for example, the rent for a room increases from USD 12 per month to around USD 20 per month if the dwelling has access to basic services such as water, electricity, and a pit latrine. Thus, real estate taxes should generally be assessed and collected by local governments. If well managed, land value taxation can be an important and buoyant revenue source for municipalities. A comprehensive land register is needed, however. Changes in land values must be monitored and the intervals for assessments (especially in periods of rapid inflation) cannot be too long.

For the poor, property taxation can mean a further obstacle to the registration of informal settlements. The poor cannot pay very much anyway, and collection will be difficult. The costs for registration of a large number of small plots and the collection of small amounts reduces revenue considerably. An alternative, especially in poorer countries, is to exempt poor settlements – at least in a first phase – and focus on establishing an effective land taxation system for wealthier landowners. This may be a manageable challenge, but the institutional capacity of local government still needs to be strengthened.

Tariff policies

Adequate service provision will never be achieved without tariffs covering the costs of operations. The poor benefit more from subsidized connection charges.

Utility operations – especially water and sewerage – are frequently a major drain on municipal resources. Illegal connections, poor collection performance and strong political resistance against setting tariffs to cover the full cost of service has made it difficult to mobilise financing for projects to serve low-income households directly. Indeed, the World Bank (1994) has estimated that the revenues of the average water enterprise in developing countries only covers about one-third of its costs. While some improvements have occurred since that study was conducted, the revenue problem for most utilities remains serious. Companies are reluctant to reveal repayment levels in newly extended piped systems in poor areas, but there are many indications that it is very low. There is significant scope for identifying and reducing 'unaccounted-for water' (including water theft and leaks) and strengthening revenue collection.

Water tariffs are often kept low in order to make them 'affordable to the poor'. However, as we have seen, in most of the cities in low-income countries, these low tariffs benefit the rich, who are the only ones connected to the network (see Basic services, p 58).

In most low-income countries, water subsidies should be used to reduce or eliminate the up-front connection/installation charge. Access to piped water is more important than the cost of municipal water. In middle income countries with near universal coverage, instruments such as increasing block tariffs (progressive and related to consumption) and cross-subsidies might be appropriate. Unfortunately, experience from such tariff systems has not been encouraging. Subsidies have often been extended to most consumers, and in this way, the system subsidized as a whole. The result is poor services in general, and for the poor in particular. The provision and pricing of water is usually a highly political issue. A financially sustainable water system with differentiated tariffs in favour of the poorest is technically and economically feasible, but in reality very difficult to establish. Increased involvement of community organizations and more transparency and accountability towards consumers may be part of the solution.

Due to the externalities involved, sanitation services, on the other hand, might merit 'across-the-board' subsidies. In theory, the 'polluter pays' principle should apply. In countries with weak enforcement mechanisms (ie most low-income countries) full cost recovery would provide a strong incentive for firms and households to use less sound sanitation solutions.

Traditional water vendor in Kolkata, India. Studies from all parts of the developing world show that the poor actually pay more to water vendors than middle and upper income households pay for their piped municipal water.

© Scanpix

However, even low-income communities are often willing to finance or build piped systems that get the sewage out of the neighbourhood. The Orangi Pilot Project in Pakistan is a good example (Box 17, p 119). Trunk sewerage and treatment usually require subsidies.

Municipalities in the capital market

Municipal borrowing is a delicate issue. Municipalities may be too inclined to increase their debt burden excessively. The risks involved should not obscure the fact that access to financial markets is a means for municipalities – including those in developing countries – to increase their opportunities to develop.

Given the difficulties that municipalities face in accessing funds on the commercial market – be it through bonds or through bank loans – more than 50 countries have established special credit intermediaries, commonly referred to as municipal development banks, to lend funds to local governments. Although some of these institutions have been around for almost three decades, they have largely remained vehicles for channelling funds from international institutions and central governments (with little emphasis on loan repayment and mobilisation of funds from capital markets). Generally, their financial performance has been poor – except for those institutions that have collateralised their loans, usually through the right to intercept transfers from the central government to the borrowing municipality. Thus, if they operate on sound commercial principles, municipal development banks can help local governments gain access to domestic capital markets.

Careful attention to the need for collateral has opened up a municipal bond market in India. In 1998, Ahmedabad became the first city to place a bond without a guarantee from the state government. The bond issue was rated AA by CRISIL, the Indian rating agency. Ahmedabad managed to achieve an investment grade rating by channelling its octroi revenues through an escrow account that is used for paying the bond holders.[25][26] A similar approach was adopted in a recent bond issue by the municipality of Douala in Cameroon.

---

25) Octroi is a tax levied on goods brought into the city. It is similar to the 'import' duties on domestically produced goods, collected at the gates to European cities in medieval times.
26) Legally, the money in the escrow account belongs to the Ahmedabad municipality. In its simplest form, an escrow account is a normal bank account controlled by a trustee ('escrow agent') who decides when and for what purpose the money may be used, based on certain criteria determined when the account was established. In this case, the rules are simple: the bond holders get paid first and the municipality receives what is left in the account.

In the Philippines, the bankers' association initiated the creation of a Local Government Units Guarantee Corporation (LGUGC), which guarantees municipal bond issues. The LGUGC charges an up-front fee of 2.5–3.5.per cent. In case of default, LGUGC assumes the debt service obligation. However, LGUGC has the right to intercept the transfers from the central government to the municipality. Since its creation in 1998, LGUGC has provided guarantees for about 20 municipal bond issues with an average size of close to USD 3 million.

Municipal utilities that are reasonably autonomous (especially in tariff setting subject to transparent and consistent regulation) and financially sound, can access local financial markets on the strength of their balance sheets and revenue flows. If they do not meet these requirements, they have to rely on mechanisms like those discussed for municipalities above.

Strengthening the capacity of local governments to effectively deliver services is a long and cumbersome process. The private sector and civil society can play active roles in building, financing, and managing infrastructure services to improve living conditions for the urban poor.

Enhancing service delivery

The need for reform and new concepts

Previous chapters have described how poor or non-existent services hamper local economic development and how unhygienic living conditions and the lack of water contribute to bad health and high rates of mortality, especially for younger children. Service delivery in many areas is still often a task for the central government and the need to decentralize the responsibility to the local level has been emphasised.

The need for reforms, however, is broader. If the quality of services is to improve, utilities must be reorganized and operations commercialised, their autonomy and financial situation strengthened, and professional management and trained staff put in place. The tariff levels must allow that operating costs are covered and maintenance and investments made possible; the collection of payments must also improve, and illegal connections and bribery must be eliminated. Tariff reforms and other measures to increase cost recovery, however, will not work if services do not improve. In the case of water, for example, it is unlikely that customers are prepared to pay for water and accept increased tariffs if the supply remains so unreliable that they still have to invest in storage tanks and maintain wells or be obliged to buy water from other sources.

The poor state of services and the obvious difficulties in undertaking the reforms that are necessary to improve public utilities have made governments and donors look for other solutions. During the 1980s, privatization or public-private partnerships (PPPs) emerged as promising option and have since been tried both in developed and developing countries. Private sector involvement has often provoked political opposition and there is no consensus on how to evaluate the outcome. Besides reports from proponents (like the WB) and opponents (like public sector unions) there is little research available. However there are many ways in which the private sector can participate and different models will probably develop in the future. In areas like transport, water and energy, it is critical that main networks, which in most cases will remain public, can function well together with a variety of private 'retail' service providers.

PPP with international firms

Public-Private Partnerships have been launched as a solution to the many problems faced by public enterprises for the provision of water and sanitation, transport, telecommunication and energy. Many contracts with international companies have been concluded. This form of 'privatization' has been highly contentious and the experiences, so far, are not conclusive.

The most visible – and controversial – form of private sector involvement in service provision has been multinational water companies managing water and sanitation facilities in cities in the developing world. Since the late 1980s, the private sector has been involved in about 300 water and/or sanitation schemes with an aggregate investment of about USD 41 billion.[27] This is commonly referred to as 'privatization' but there is a broad range of approaches for what in reality are public-private partnerships (Box 16).

The most common form of private participation in the water sector is the concession model. All major water 'privatizations' have been of this type. Complete divestitures are rare since the government usually continues to own some shares in the utility. Build-operate-transfer (BOT) contracts generally involve construction of new water or sewerage treatment facilities. In money terms, nearly two-thirds of the BOT projects are in East Asia. In countries where the water utilities have been financially weak – as in Sub-Saharan Africa, Eastern Europe and the former Soviet Union – private participation has typically taken the form of management or lease contracts. (Figure 10)

Studies of the impact of private participation in the water sector in countries as different as Argentina, Côte d'Ivoire and the Palestinian West Bank have shown that performance of the utility generally improved: productivity has gone up and water losses were reduced (Estache et al 2000, Kerf et al 1998, Kessides 2004, Kikeri and Nellis 2004).[28]

Service coverage also appears to have improved, but extensions to previously unserved areas have been less than was hoped. This depends critically on the regulatory regime and the extent of new investments. Unfortu-

27) All figures in this section are from the World Bank's online PPI database. Investment figures include all committed investments in projects with private participation. Equity contributions and loans from public sector entities (including loans from the multilateral development banks and export credit agencies) are included and not only financing from private sector investors and lenders. Furthermore, the investment figures for some individual projects also include committed future investments during the concession period, which may or may not materialize. The investments actually undertaken by private enterprises are lower than USD 41 billion.

28) The PPPs are often associated with water sector reforms and funding (eg WB loans) for new investments. The outcome is a combined effect of all factors, making it difficult to evaluate the impact of "privatization" alone.

Management contracts. A private contractor has responsibility for day-to-day operations and routine maintenance. The public enterprise owns the assets and finances any new investments. The contractor is normally responsible for billing and collection but the owner controls the revenues. Typically, the contracts have performance incentives, but most of the commercial risk rests with the owner.

Lease contracts. The public enterprise owns the assets and is responsible for capital investment but leases the facility to a private contractor who pays a fee for the right to operate the assets. The operator's own staff operates and maintains the facility and undertakes all billing and collection. (If the enterprise makes a loss, the lease fee can be replaced by a payment to the operator.)

Concessions. The public sector continues to own the assets, but transfers responsibility for both financing of new facilities and daily operations and maintenance to the private concessionaire. The concessionaire collects the revenues from the consumers to cover its capital and operating costs. At the end of the concession period (20-30 years), the concessionaire returns the assets to the public sector, or the concession is renewed.

Build-Operate-Transfer contracts (BOT). The public sector entity enters into a long-term contract with the private party which finances, builds and operates a facility for a certain number of years. At the end of the contract period, ownership of the assets is transferred to the government. The BOT model is best suited for large facilities such as water or sewage treatment plants and investment in greenfield projects.

Divestitures. Ownership of the assets with full responsibility for capital investment, operations, and maintenance is transferred to the private company. The investor takes on the market, legal, regulatory, and operating risks.

nately, it is only recently that attention has been given to the need for explicit strategies to extend services to poor urban households.

Although results have been relatively positive, private participation is no panacea for solving the water and sanitation problems of most developing countries. First of all, the global water companies have changed their strategies since the mid-1990s and the amount of money committed has fallen steadily from USD 8.4 billion in 1997 to USD 0.9 billion in 2003.[29] Most important, however, is their reluctance to take the risk associated with investments in low-income countries. In these countries they prefer management and lease contracts, where they are not required to make any significant investments (Table 9). Thus, the public sector will continue to bear the main burden for urban infrastructure investments in low-income countries. However, engaging the private sector under management or lease

---

29) Commitments not only from private enterprises. See previous footnote.

contracts such as in Gaza, Mozambique and Uganda can potentially result in significantly better performance of the water utility.

Private participation in water and sanitation has been highly contentious. Several schemes, particularly in Latin America, have been contested and targeted in popular protests against globalisation. One example is the water concession in Cochabamba, Bolivia, where violent political demonstrations led to the cancellation of the contract. Concessions in the water sector experience more serious problems than in telecommunications and power. Around 7 per cent of all projects with private participation have either been cancelled or are under arbitration, including the three largest (Buenos Aires, Manila and Indah, Malaysia).

There are several reasons why private water projects experience difficulties.[30] One reason is unrealistic expectations following the 'selling' of private participation as a quick and painless remedy to severe problems faced in most systems. Weak regulation and poor contract design have also contributed to the problem, as have external shocks in the form of large devaluations (Manila and Buenos Aires).

Private local service providers

The potential of local enterprises has probably been overlooked, although many private service providers already exist.

Local, small-scale entrepreneurs have long played an important role in providing water to low and middle-income families in developing countries. Most urban poor are still served by water vendors with push carts and trucks. Where groundwater conditions are favourable, it is also common that the owner of a well sells water to his neighbours.

An interesting development is the emergence of private entrepreneurs who own and operate piped water networks. In Kampala, Uganda, a private company has built two small networks since 1995. These networks include both standpipes and house connections. In Cambodia, outside Phnom Penh and Sihanoukville, almost all new investments in water supply networks have been made by local private investors, ranging from a few thousand dollars for villages of a few hundred families to USD 900 000 for the provincial town of Banteay Meanchey (population 100 000 in 2000). Such operators exist in all regions although they seem to be most common in Latin America. Some 400 *aguateros* operating piped networks from their own wells serve around 900 000 people in Paraguay.

Small-scale operators can play an important role in serving both inner

---

30) See, for example, Harris, Clive, Hodges, John, Schur, Michael and Shukla, Padmesh (2003) 'Infrastructure Projects—A Review of Cancelled Private Projects', Note 252 in the series *Public Policy for the Private Sector*, World Bank, Washington, DC.

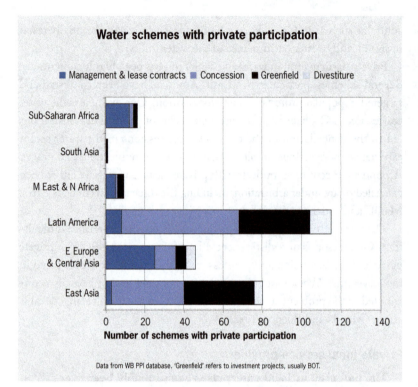

Water schemes with private participation

■ Management & lease contracts ■ Concession ■ Greenfield ▫ Divestiture

Sub-Saharan Africa

South Asia

M East & N Africa

Latin America

E Europe
& Central Asia

East Asia

0   20   40   60   80   100   120   140
Number of schemes with private participation

Data from WB PPI database. 'Greenfield' refers to investment projects, usually BOT.

FIGURE 10.
Water schemes with private participation have been more common in Latin America and East Asia. Investments are also concentrated to these regions, while management and lease contracts dominate in other parts of the world.

Table 9. Country income level and private participation in water supply and sanitation

	INCOME LEVEL		
	Low income	Lower middle	Upper middle
Type of PPI (Number of Schemes)			
Management contract	3	12	5
Lease contract	7	6	20
Concession	0	49	62
Greenfield project	5	36	42
Divestiture	0	5	15
Total	15	108	144
Investments (USD Millions)			
Government assets	10	830	4300
New facilities	610	15280	18880
Total investments	620	16110	21180
Investments per capita (USD)	0.3	6.9	47

Data from WB PPI database.

city slums and peri-urban areas. Unfortunately, the legal and regulatory framework often works against them. The state-owned water utility typically has a legal monopoly on providing water within the whole city, including peri-urban areas. Thus, small-scale providers may be actively opposed by the authorities or face the risk of expropriation. Small providers instead should be encouraged and regulated with 'a light touch' to enable them to adopt cost-effective design standards and collect fees that yield a competitive return on their capital. However, there are risks involved: small providers may sell contaminated water and a system to control quality must be in place.

Community-based alternatives

Without adequate services and with no hope that the situation would improve within a foreseeable future, poor communities have often been forced to develop their own solutions.

Around the world, there are examples of neighbourhood water supply systems managed through NGOs and community-based organizations concerned with slum upgrading and other shelter related activities. The Orangi Pilot Project in Pakistan and the Parivartan scheme in India illustrate both the diversity of approaches and some of the common elements of success.

SEWA started as a union of self-employed women in the Indian state of Gujarat. It moved into micro-finance through the SEWA bank and established the Mahila Housing SEWA Trust (MHT) in 1994. SEWA Bank and MHT took the initiative to the Parivartan upgrading scheme in Ahmedabad, a city of five million people. The Parivartan scheme is a partnership between the community, the Ahmedabad Municipal Corporation and the private sector, each of which pay one-third of the cost. The project comprises a package of seven on-site infrastructure services including paved roads, individual toilets, water and drainage connections and street lighting.

Box 17: The famous OPP

The Orangi Pilot Project (OPP) started in 1980 to improve sanitation in one of Karachi's *katachi abadis* with a population around one million. Initially it was met with indifference – if not hostility – by the municipal authorities. However, over time it established a constructive relationship with the water utility and the city's slum upgrading agency. Thus, while OPP organized community construction of on-site sewerage pipes, the city built the main sewerage trunks. This model has now been widely adopted in Pakistan. OPP has gradually expanded into other activities with a direct impact on the lives of slum dwellers and is working with NGOs and community organizations in other cities of Pakistan.

The **Community-Led Infrastructure Finance Facility, CLIFF,** is a fund that has been designed to act as a catalyst in slum upgrading. It provides support for community initiatives to improve housing or infrastructure with the potential for scaling up. The idea is to increase access of poor urban communities to commercial and public sector finance for medium to large-scale infrastructure and housing initiatives. The financing facility provides loans, guarantees and technical assistance to support a range of project including new housing, community-managed resettlement programmes and public toilet blocks. Bridging loans are available for kick-starting large infrastructure and resettlement projects, with the funding recovered from the government.

CLIFF is funded by UK and Sweden and implemented by Homeless International, a UK NGO. The intention is to work in countries in all regions, but the first initiative is in India with participation of SPARC, the National Slum Dwellers federation and Mahila Milan (Women's Cooperatives).

Main functions of CLIFF are:
- to provide bridging loans, guarantees and technical assistance
- to initiate medium scale urban rehabilitation in cities in the South
- to work in partnership with community-based organizations and NGOs who have, or can be assisted to develop, a track record in delivery of urban rehabilitation
- to seek to attract commercial, local and public sector finance for further schemes and thus be able to scale up the activities
- to establish local CLIFF agencies as lasting institutions.

MHT mobilises the slum communities to participate in the upgrading process and to pay their portion of the total cost. SEWA Bank and MHT are actively preparing similar schemes in other Indian cities.

The most important element of success is clearly that they are driven 'from the bottom up' and that the programmes respond to the real needs of the slum dwellers. But success and scaling-up also depend critically on the ability of these organizations to gain support from the municipal authorities. The Orangi example also illustrates the growing cooperation among NGOs.

'Local funds' appear to be a promising vehicle for governments and donors to encourage and support grassroots initiatives. The Urban Community Development Office (UCDO) of Thailand was set up in 1992 as an autonomous unit, with a revolving fund of 1 250 million Baht (about USD 50 million at the time). The Government of Thailand intended to address urban poverty on a national scale. The objectives were to improve living conditions and increase the organizational capacity of urban poor communities through the promotion of savings and credit groups, and the provision of 'wholesale' loans to community organizations at favourable interest rates. The money was either on-lent to the members for house improvements or income earn-

Network repair in Outi, India. Urban areas depend on functioning transport, communication, electrical supply and many other services. Utilities often operate with losses, because tariffs are set too low. Poor maintenance and limited investments are inevitable consequences. Fundamental reforms are often required.

© Göran Tannerfeldt

The municipality of San Pedro Almolonga in Guatemala with 15 000 inhabitants, mostly Maya, decided to take care of its solid waste. The problem was that horticulture and the market produced a lot of organic waste. However, it was only when the municipality got technical assistance and a loan from Fideicomiso para el Desarollo Local (FDLG), supported by Sida, that they could develop a project to solve the problem.

With a truck to collect waste and a plant where it is sorted and separated, the waste is now well managed. Glass, plastics and paper are recycled, and the organic material is composted and becomes a fertiliser. Both are sold and the income helps to cover investment and running costs.

Thirty per cent of the total investment cost, roughly USD 415 000, was covered by a loan from FDLG. The municipality contributed 27 per cent and the rest was financed from regional and governmental sources.

The case of San Pedro Almolonga shows that even a small municipality can take action to improve environmental sustainability. It also shows that a small loan to a municipality could trigger funding from other, domestic sources.

ing investments, or used for implementation of community improvements. In July 2000, UCDO become the Community Organization Development Institute (CODI). CODI is placed directly under the Ministry of Finance, but with a highly decentralized structure to maintain its responsiveness to the needs of the poor. CODI has now been given the lead role in implementation of the Thai government's nation-wide Baan Mankong programme, which seeks to provide secure tenure to and upgrade the neighbourhoods of some 300 000 households between 2003 and 2007.

In the local development programme Prodel in Nicaragua the communities are involved in the definition, implementation, financing and maintenance of local infrastructure works in collaboration with the municipalities (Box 4, p 41).

The cases cited above demonstrate how households, communities, NGOs, municipalities and central governments can cooperate. In OPP there is household finance and community management. In Parivartan financing is from households/micro finance agencies and with municipal management. In the case of UDCO the state is financing improvements and the communities take care of management. In Nicaragua the financing is shared, the municipalities are responsible, but the households are involved in all stages. The variety is probably a result of different conditions in each case, but it is also an indication that, in spite of successful examples, established models still remain to be developed.

Housing development in all parts of the world is a combination of public and private investment financed with long-term loans. In most developing countries the financial services is this area are poor, and not adapted to the needs and demands of low-income households. This demand can be met if conditions of loans and deposits are appropriately designed.

Creating functioning housing finance services

The challenge to eliminate slums and prevent the formation of new slums cannot be met unless governments at all levels adopt comprehensive housing policies which adequately address the problems. Such policies must build on an enabling concept, involving the stakeholders and mobilising available resources. In many countries of the developing world there is no policy at all. The financing of land, infrastructure, shelter and basic services is a key issue and in most developing countries, the lack of functioning housing finance services is a prime limitation.

The role of the formal finance sector

Some mortgage lenders have started to address the needs of low-income borrowers. The Housing Development Finance Company (HDFC), the leading private sector mortgage lender in India, relies on NGOs and self-help groups to channel loans to low-income families. HDFC had experienced a recovery rate of nearly 100 per cent on such loans. The Housing and Urban Development Company (HUDCO) of the Government of India finances a variety of schemes, including sites and services schemes and core housing, where large percentages of the houses to be constructed are reserved for people with low incomes. Birla Home Finance, India, has a new scheme that targets poor urban households with monthly incomes less than INR 6 000 (about USD 135).

In South Africa, the National Urban Reconstruction and Housing Agency (Nurcha) has adopted an even more innovative approach. It supports housing projects for people eligible for the government capital subsidy by providing guarantees on working capital and bridge financing to developers, especially emerging developers. It also supports institutions producing rental housing for low-income households. Clearly, Nurcha's operation is not typical of other Sub-Saharan African countries, where financial institutions are in very early stages of development.

Traditional mortgage instruments tend to be inflexible and not suited to incremental housing, ie when people build their houses in stages, which is common practice. There is also a growing awareness that traditional mortgage loans might not be attractive to the urban poor, even if they could obtain such loans. Most slum dwellers not only have low incomes, but also suffer from a high degree of income insecurity. Thus, they can ill afford fixed monthly mortgage payments and face the risk of losing their home in case of temporary loss of income. High transaction costs, often totally out of proportion to the loan amount, is another reason why traditional mortgage loans are unaffordable. However, the situation varies from country to country and in some countries it is possible to use the mortgage instrument also for loans to poor households.

Housing cooperatives are a potentially very suitable model for low-income households. In countries where such institutions are well established they act as developers, creating complete housing areas for their members. It is also an attractive model because it is based on savings. For the very poor, who only can afford incremental housing and very basic services, the housing cooperatives may not be an option.

For workers with stable incomes it is sometimes possible to get housing through employers or through programmes based on salary deductions. In some cases employees are offered a kind of lease arrangement – an initial rental arrangement which may after a number of years be converted to ownership. Such arrangements, however, risk creating dependence on the employer. The lease model may also be used by an independent developer.

Micro-finance for housing

Poor people can not afford a complete new house. When they have acquired a plot with reasonable security of tenure, they build as much as they can afford, and then add to this. For these millions of households, a micro-credit for housing is then a highly enabling option.

Unable to obtain mortgage loans, the urban poor have relied on household savings, loans from family and friends, credit from suppliers of building material and whatever other sources they can find. Starting with the most basic shack built of temporary materials, they gradually expand and improve – a process that can take many years. The rate of construction and the amount of money spent over time depend not only on the income and savings of the family but also on the level of tenure security.

In recent years, a new option has become available to some of the urban poor: small loans for home improvements from micro-finance institutions

(MFIs) such as Grameen Bank in Bangladesh, the Self-Employed Women's Association (SEWA) Bank in India, the National Co-operative Housing Union (NACHU) in Kenya, or Mibanco in Peru and FUNDEVI in Honduras. Most of these organizations are general micro-finance institutions (serving micro-enterprises) while a few, such as NACHU, were originally set up to provide housing loans. The majority of them provide credits directly to clients. Others, like PRODEL in Nicaragua and FDLG in Guatemala, provide 'wholesale' financing to micro-finance institutions, which in turn supply 'retail' finance for housing improvements to households.

Micro housing finance represents an evolution of the model for lending to micro-enterprises. Traditionally, these institutions have provided small, short-term loans only for 'productive' purposes. Home improvement loans were seen initially as business investments linked to the use of homes as workplaces – an implicit recognition of one of the most direct ways in which housing can be a productive asset. Increasingly, the micro-finance institutions have developed housing loans into a separate line of business. Mibanco, for example, has started a separate programme, *Micasa*, for housing loans (Box 20). Some, like SEWA Bank, spend much effort on community organization (where deposit-taking and lending are instruments in this process), project development and in advocacy with municipalities and government agencies. Others, like Banco Sol in Bolivia, operate more like traditional mortgage lenders and do require a lien (legal claim) on the property for larger loans.

Housing-related loans typically have a longer term than loans for working capital. This reduces the opportunity for micro-finance institutions to on-lend existing funds rapidly, and they are constrained by the availability of medium term capital. Most of the micro-housing finance lenders are not well integrated into the financial sector, and they tend to rely on member savings for their lending activities, supplemented by donor contributions that are lent and relent. Thus, many of the best known actors operate on a relatively limited scale. SEWA Bank has a housing finance portfolio of about USD 900 000. The Homeless People's Federation of the Philippines (HPFP) has assets of about USD 700 000 and NACHU 'recycles' about USD 600 000 in funds once received from USAID and the Ford Foundation. A few institutions, however, have been able to overcome the capital constraint and reach significant scale in their housing finance operations. Mibanco, with a housing portfolio of USD 15 million, and Grameen Bank with USD 20 million are two examples.

A major constraint of shelter micro-finance is the individual nature of the lending, which makes it suitable for home improvement but not for other important needs. Loans for land purchase, neighbourhood development and infrastructure are usually not available.

A sound strategy for increasing the access of the poor to housing finance must follow a two-pronged approach: the formal housing finance institutions need to move down to reach lower income groups, and the scale of operations of the micro-housing finance institutions should be expanded. It is important for housing finance in general, and also for the micro-finance sector, that the cadastral systems improve.

In all cases, it is essential that the institutions are financially sound and operate on a commercial basis, and that they are able to access capital markets to extend their operations. Interest rates should reflect the true cost of the lending operation. Donors can facilitate the expansion of the micro-housing finance sector through instruments like USAID's partial guarantee, which enabled Mibanco to access the local bond market, through grants that increase the institution's capital base, or through loans to micro-lenders (as Sida is doing in Central America). Donor support in the form of grants or subsidized loans, however, always runs the risk of distorting market conditions, and has to be handled with care if a sound and competitive micro-finance sector is to develop.

Rebuilding after Hurricane Mitch in Honduras. Most houses in the developing world are built by people themselves. Simple shacks are gradually expanded and improved over time. With affordable loans this process can go faster and with better building quality.

© Kina Robberts

Subsidies for housing

Housing subsidies are justified, but have a poor track record. Often they have benefited less poor groups. Subsidized interests rates became a burden for the budget and subsidies to construction companies benefited them rather than the households. However, there are well-designed subsidy schemes. Poor countries should subsidize infrastructure, services and the provision of land rather than the construction of shelter.

Most housing subsidy programmes in developing countries have been costly and have had little effect on living conditions for the great majority of the urban poor. A recent study of the direct and indirect housing subsidies in Morocco showed that they exceeded 2.2 per cent of GDP and, because they were poorly targeted, largely failed to benefit the urban poor (le Blanc, 2005).

Traditionally, the most common form of housing subsidy has been interest rate subsidies provided by public sector housing banks or through directed lending schemes. Since in most developing countries the poor have little prospect of getting a mortgage loan, such schemes tend to benefit only high-income groups.

Another approach taken by governments is to build rental housing for 'low income' groups. Such schemes have typically been associated with inefficient and costly construction, inadequate maintenance and corruption, both in construction and selection of tenants. Universally, such programmes have been too small (due largely to their high production costs and poor rent collection, which has made them a financial drain on the national budget) and have failed to have any significant impact on the housing market.

Capital subsidies can generally be better targeted at the urban poor and at the same time help promote efficient construction by the private sector. The best known example of such a programme is the combined saving-subsidy-loan system that was introduced in Chile in the late 1970s. Criteria for obtaining the capital subsidy were the amount saved and the period of saving together with social indicators (like number of children). The system defined several categories of housing aiming at different income groups. The smaller and cheaper houses were more subsidized, favouring the poor. The balance of the cost of a house was met by the household saving and non-subsidized mortgage loan from a private bank.

Annually, private developers were invited to tender at fixed prices for a certain number of houses and were selected through competitive bidding. Developers had to provide the land, the infrastructure and the planning of the area, and were selected on the basis of the qualities of the offered housing.

Chile's housing policy, as briefly described above, is comprehensive and offers several advantages. A number of subsidies for each category of housing are allocated annually in the budget. The amount is known and the system does not imply any future claims on the budget. The role of the government is limited. The production is entirely market-based and has promoted competition and rational production building. The rules for the households are clear and stable and the outcome of long-term saving predictable. The allocation of subsidies is transparent and there is a possibility to appeal. However, the system has also been criticised because the low-income housing was often located too far away from the centre and transport facilities were not developed at the same time.

Similar programmes, though less sophisticated, have been implemented in a few other countries, such as South Africa and Costa Rica. The programmes tend to be costly if they are to have any significant impact. In Chile, for example, the annual cost in the early 1980s was around 2 per cent of GDP. Most low-income countries lack both the financial resources and the administrative capacity to manage such programmes in a transparent and efficient manner.

Government expenditures to subsidize basic infrastructure, land and secure tenure are efficient means to improve housing conditions for the urban poor and an option for more comprehensive housing subsidies. Government intervention is particularly useful here, since the communities alone cannot do much to solve these problems, while they are able to build basic shelter themselves.

The most cost-effective government interventions to make adequate housing more affordable appear to be policy and regulatory changes aimed at improving the functioning of land and housing markets.

Experience has shown that inappropriate policies, cumbersome procedures and unrealistic standards impose heavy costs on the poor. In Mumbai, for example, the Urban Land Ceiling Act and a host of other regulations, combined with bureaucratic inertia, limited the supply of urbanized land to such an extent that in early 1996, the city had higher land prices than Tokyo or New York (Payne 1998).[31] Mumbai is in no way unique.[32] Analyses of housing markets in Asia and Latin America (Mayo 1999, WB 1993) have shown that countries with over-regulated, unresponsive housing supply systems (ie Mexico and Malaysia) have housing prices that are twice as high as in countries with un-bureaucratic, flexible supply systems (Chile and Thailand).

---

31) The Urban Land Ceiling Act restricted the ownership of land to 500 sq.m. (for both individuals and corporations). This prevented private enterprises from developing housing on any reasonable scale and gave people incentives to "hide" the real ownership of land (and thus dried up land transactions and the "supply" of land for development by either households or corporations).

32) Prices of developed land on the urban fringe in Latin American Cities exceed those for similar areas in developed countries. Smolka (2002)

What could be more important for governments in development countries than to facilitate opportunities for the majority of the population to earn their living?

Enabling a livelihood

Informal is normal

Urban development policies often appear to be based on concepts and visions that are far from reality; they ignore or disregard the conditions of the majority of the citizens.

Employment is expected to mean a fixed job with a safe salary; housing is supposed to mean dwellings with pre-set standards and solid building materials; water should come through the pipe, and flush toilets should be connected to a water-borne sewerage system. Those who do not have a salaried formal employment and live in shacks with no piped water are classified as 'jobless' and 'homeless'.

In reality, poor people do have some kind of a livelihood, everybody lives somewhere and no one survives without water. The problem is that the means developed by poor households for survival are not recognized by the authorities. Instead of supporting the efforts of the poor, governments either turn to repressive policies – clearing slums and harassing hawkers, or to unrealistic 'providing' policies – to 'create' jobs and build houses and infrastructure. However, the governments' resources for employing, housing and providing water to the growing number of urban poor are limited. And even with the best intentions, conventional approaches tend to be unaffordable and in the end they rarely benefit the poor.

Governments instead need to come to terms with the realities that the majority of their citizens face daily, they need to listen to their views on how different obstacles could be removed or overcome. Then they need to adopt an enabling approach aiming at facilitating poor people's own efforts to improve their living conditions.

A first step, however, would be to recognize that the informal is normal. Their cities rely on the informal economy. It represents 50-70 per cent of total employment and often the majority of their citizens live in slums and informal settlements.

The tiny Central Watch Clinic and Mobile Phone Repair service is located between Paradise Café and Miami Wines and Spirits. Micro-businesses in Kibera slum area, Nairobi.

© Magnus Rosshagen

Pro-poor policies

Local governments can do a lot to reduce the costs and risks of working informally.

The informal economy generates income for a large number of people, both employed and self-employed. Equally important, it provides essential services for the urban poor at a cost they can afford. The informal economy should be seen as part of the national economy, and not as a social problem or a matter of law and order, which is too often the case now. Improving the conditions of this informal economy and increasing its contribution to economic development benefiting the poor would be more appropriate.

Local governments can do a lot to reduce the costs and risks of working informally. Regulations which prohibit or restrict home-based businesses should be revised. Street traders should be accepted and have space allocated to them. The very useful work of waste pickers and scavengers should be recognized and their working conditions improved – especially with regard to health and safety. The approach should be enabling and not imposing unrealistic restrictions. In order to understand and be able to respond to the needs and concerns of the informal economy, the authorities should support organizations of informal sector workers, and establish dialogue and working partnerships with them.

The construction sector is important because it employs a lot of semi-skilled and unskilled workers. But it is also a key sector for the economy as a whole and could contribute more to economic development both locally and at a national level. Enabling policies for housing, infrastructure and the construction industry in general are therefore strategic.

Employment of unskilled labour can in some cases be promoted through labour-based methods for infrastructure works. Construction may be organized and contracted in different ways and with different employment effects. The use of small community-based contractors creates local employment and may reduce costs. Slum improvement projects offer the opportunity to employ the inhabitants themselves and thus improve living conditions and income at the same time.

Urban agriculture could mean commercial production of vegetables, fruit and other high-price crops, or small livestock (like poultry) within or close to the city. It could also mean small-scale farming in back yards. Urban agriculture is just a small share of total agricultural production, but it can make a significant contribution to livelihood and health of many urban poor. The policy issue is to facilitate urban agriculture for the poor. Particularly important is allowing and encouraging it on publicly owned land not presently being used. Relaxed local regulation is also needed.

Financial services for the poor

Low-income households and people running micro-businesses need insurance, loans, savings accounts and other financial services on terms and conditions that are adapted to them.

In many developing countries financial services are not well developed. The commercial banks are often small and offer a limited range of services to a limited range of clients within a limited geographic area. The formal banking sector has, in general, been uninterested in developing services adapted to small and micro-enterprises, the self-employed, and low-income households even though these represent a growing and potentially important market.

Governments and actors in the financial sector have, in general, not realized that poor people and the informal economy need financial services such as credit, saving and insurance. These services have to some extent already developed in the informal economy. Loans have been provided by individuals or community associations, which also have managed saving for funerals and other expenses and provided help in case of illness or death.

Governments have often regarded private lending not as a service but as exploitation. The informal sector bankers – 'loan sharks' – and their activities have been prohibited in legislation. This did not stop the business, but instead resulted in higher interest rates to cover the greater risk. As in other areas, the authorities have again failed to understand the real need. They have undertaken actions which may have been well-meant, but which actually resulted in things becoming worse for the poor.

Since the 1980s, micro-finance has grown in response to the need of the informal economy for small loans on suitable terms. Grameen Bank in Bangladesh, a pioneer, was given early support by Sweden. Micro-finance institutions usually have developed from NGOs and been supported by donors.

Today micro-finance has developed into an important industry. Demand is reportedly still far from satisfied, and the sustainability of the institutions – particularly with respect to the capacity to capture additional capital – is still an issue. The donor community has had a leading role in the development of the sector. CGAP (Consultative Group to Assist the Poor), a multi-donor consortium in the World Bank, has served as a service centre to the entire micro-finance industry, but it has also provided guidelines setting standards for financial management aiming at commercial viability. CGAP has also strongly influenced the international policy for development and expansion of micro-finance. In short, the objective is to integrate micro-finance into the formal financial sector. This would make it sustainable on commercial terms and reduce (and ultimately elimi-

nate) dependence on donor funding. It is expected that in this way greater demands could be met. Part of the strategy is that micro-finance institutions would be regulated and supervised by the regulatory authorities. This should strengthen their capacity to act in the financial markets and also allow them to offer new services like deposits and savings. Several micro-finance institutions like Banco Sol in Bolivia and Mibanco in Peru transformed themselves into formal banks during the 1990s.

Transformation into a bank raises the costs however, because of regulatory requirements. Since the administrative costs for small and short-term credits are already high, and the handling of very small savings accounts for poor people is even more costly, there is a risk of 'mission drift', ie a tendency to focus on less poor clients.

National governments in some countries have been reluctant to welcome NGOs with micro-finance activities. High interest rates – explained by the administrative costs of small loans – have been questioned, and in Nicaragua the government introduced limits on these rates. It was only the introduction of other charges to be paid by the clients that allowed the institutions to survive.

Governments should realize that micro-finance is an essential service and facilitate its development by removing obstacles, promoting competition, and establishing a stable regulatory framework. There are also other options, for example, to require banks to direct a portion of their lending to under-served groups. For formal banks, a system of loans to community groups, as in India, is interesting since the amounts would be larger and the group is responsible for dealing with individual members. In micro-finance 'community banks' have proven to be effective in reaching the poorest and particularly attractive for women.

To conclude, micro-finance is important for the informal economy and for the livelihood of the urban poor. Directly, because small enterprises, besides providing an income to the owners, also employ a large number of people (Table 3, p 50); indirectly, because the micro-enterprises provide goods and services to the poor communities at affordable prices.

●

FURTHER READING
UN-HABITAT (2005) *Financing Urban Shelter: Global Report on Human Settlements 2005*, Earthscan, London
Mitlin, Diana and Satterthwaite, David (2004) *Empowering Squatter Citizen: Local Government, Civil Society and Urban Poverty Reduction*, Earthscan, London
Winblad, Uno and Simpson-Hébert, Mayling (2004) *Ecological Sanitation*, SEI, Stockholm
Kessides, Ioannis N (2004) *Reforming Infrastructure – Privatization, Regulation, and Competition*, World Bank, Washington DC and Oxford University Press, Oxford
de Soto, Hernando (1989) *The Other Path: The invisible revolution in the Third World*, I B Taurus, London

Key areas in pro-poor urban development

Governance and urban management

✓ decentralization policies, local self-governance, democracy at the local level

✓ transparent and efficient municipal administration, measures against corruption

✓ comprehensive and inclusive local development strategies (involving all stake-holders, including economic development, land use, infrastructure, environment, culture etc)

✓ pro-poor policy and broadened opportunities for participation by the poor

✓ land management, in particular to ensure the provision of serviced land for housing, cadastral systems, physical planning

✓ strengthening of municipal finance

Infrastructure and basic services

✓ reforming of public utilities including regulatory frameworks, tariff structures and the promotion of market-oriented and demand-driven approaches to service provision

✓ enabling of private sector participation, especially local firms and community initiatives

✓ development of affordable solutions to water, sanitation and energy in poor settlements including subsidized connection fees for the poor.

✓ urban transport, especially non-motorised traffic and public transports

Housing and slum upgrading

✓ housing policy

✓ secure tenure, legalisation of squatter settlements

✓ revision of obsolete planning and building regulation

✓ improved land and housing markets

✓ legal protection of tenants

✓ promotion of self-construction and incremental housing

✓ housing finance including micro-finance for low-income households

✓ integrated improvement of slum areas

✓ education and health facilities even in informal settlements

Environment

✓ improved sanitary conditions through better infrastructure and service delivery

✓ reduction of air pollution

✓ waste water treatment and industrial waste water management, ecological sanitation

✓ solid waste management and promotion of recycling concepts

✓ management of the historic environment including its protection and sustainable use

✓ 'greening of the city'

✓ energy conservation, particularly with regard to heating of housing and the use of renewable energy sources

✓ education and information on health and environment

Local economic development

✓ promote efficiency in the economy through improved infrastructure and service provision and through removal of obstacles and disincentives such as obsolete regulations and corruption.

✓ enabling environment for self-employment and micro-enterprises

✓ pro-poor financial services

✓ employment generation, eg labour-intensive methods for infrastructure works

✓ urban agriculture

Safety and health

✓ prevention of crime through institutional development, training of the police and support to neighbourhood actions

✓ inclusion of youth and support to youth activities

✓ storm water drainage to prevent landslides and other measures to reduce damage caused by hurricanes, earthquakes, etc

✓ safer environment for women like lighting of walkways, improved public transport, etc

✓ improved traffic safety

✓ risk reduction as part of urban planning and management

✓ programmes to prevent the spreading of HIV/AIDS

✓ accessibility for disabled

5.

THE ROLE OF DEVELOPMENT COOPERATION

Towns and cities in the developing world need support to combat poverty, eliminate slums and halt pollution of air and water. The donor community cannot continue turning a blind eye to the growing urban crisis in the poorest countries of the world.

*Why should cities in the developing world need external assistance,
if they are 'engines of economic development'? Or, why should they be
supported, if they are a source of human misery?*

Rationale for support to urban development

A vision of hope

We have seen that urban population growth in poor countries will continue. It has also been shown that urbanization is a transition from a predominantly agrarian society into a more diversified economy, which then becomes more and more integrated into the global networks of trade, communication and finance.

This structural change – or in other words, economic development – is the driving force behind urbanization; economic development without urbanization has never occurred anywhere. It is not yet universally recognized that this diversification is positive also for agriculture, forestry and fisheries and thus for the rural population thanks to growing markets, improved services and alternative occupation opportunities.

Chapters two and three described how rapid urban growth is accompanied by serious problems. The misery in which the poorest live, and the mushrooming of slums and squatter camps, have all contributed to a negative image of urbanization in developing countries and have spurred policies to contain migration. Such policies not only ignore the fact that natural population increase is the overriding cause of urban growth, but also hamper social and economic development.

There is an 'urban development paradox' since urban centres offer opportunities and advantages and are economic and cultural 'engines of development' at the same time as they are centres of human misery and environmental degradation. However, the problems are not inherent to urbanization as such or to the size of urban centres; most importantly, they can be addressed.

In the long term the increased productivity of the urban economy covers the costs of urban infrastructure and services. In the short term the task is difficult due to human, institutional and financial constraints during a period of rapid change.

For development cooperation, this long-term perspective is important: a positive and sustained development is possible and support should 'go with the flow' and help to release those developmental forces that are stronger than any effect of external aid.

The magnitude of urban problems is challenging, but they are no more daunting than many other development challenges. Urban development cooperation is also facilitated by several factors:

The spatial concentration makes implementation and monitoring of projects and programmes easier. The population is relatively young, educated and less tradition-bound, which contributes to a dynamic environment in favour of change.

Numerous examples prove that good urban governance together with capable urban management can confront the challenges of poverty and population growth. International cooperation can help the cities and towns of developing countries to find the path towards sustainable development, and to improve conditions for the poor during what is always a difficult transition. The investments to eliminate slums and the need for external funding are not prohibitive – as described in 'Funding needs' (p 161).

Strategic reasons for urban development cooperation

A strategy for urban development is also a strategy for national and international development, since it will address determining factors for social and economic development. External support is needed and can play an important role.

Seven strategic reasons for specific and increased support to urban development by the donor community are:

1. Developing countries are becoming more urbanized, and urban conditions will determine future economic, cultural and social development.

2. Urban poverty is a serious and growing problem. Poverty is being urbanized. Improving conditions for at least 100 million slum dwellers by year 2020 is a target of the Millennium Development Goals.

3. Serious environmental problems have to be addressed in urban areas. Some are associated with poverty, others with economic growth and new consumption patterns. Cities are major polluters, as well as major consumers of natural resources often disrupting ecological circuits.

4. Up to two-thirds of the GDP of most countries is generated in major urban centres. Urban infrastructure, planning and land use, regulations and governance – all have a great impact on the urban economy – small and informal enterprises in particular. Efficiently run cities promote economic development.

5. Urban development is also crucial for the future of rural areas. Rural development requires the services that are only provided in the towns. But economic development of rural areas is also dependent on the growing demand by town dwellers for agricultural products. This, together with rural-urban migration, actually raises rural per capita income. Transfers from town dwellers are also a significant input.

6. Cultural development – media and communication, educational opportunities and human interaction and innovation – originates in urban centres, but is of vital importance for development of the country as a whole.

7. Prevalence rates of HIV/AIDS are particularly serious in urban areas, and are a threat to development in general.

Poor countries need support to fulfil the Millennium Development Goals (MDGs) and to meet the challenges of rapid urban growth. Such support would address strategic issues of international development, but is still not high on the development cooperation agenda. In contrast to rural development, few donor agencies have defined urban development as a priority area and most agencies have no 'institutional home' for this.

The particular features and conditions of urban areas have been overlooked in development cooperation, which either tends to have a sector-specific approach or a focus on rural conditions.

Some have argued that support always has had an urban bias, that resources 'end up in towns anyway'. This is too simple: a teacher training college serves primary education in rural areas and a cargo terminal in the main port benefits the whole economy. And even if projects are managed from urban areas, few are aimed to improve the urban situation per se, and so rarely make a difference for the urban poor.

Sometimes it is assumed that development cooperation to improve conditions in urban areas would encourage migration, while rural development would be expected to reduce migration. In fact rural development and urban development both stimulate migration.

The Millennium Development Goals, the Habitat Agenda and the Paris Declaration are the cornerstones of the international policy framework for development cooperation towards urban development.

Policy framework

International commitments

All international development efforts are guided by the Millennium Declaration and the *Millennium Development Goals* (MDG). The contents are described in box 21.

The internationally adopted policy framework includes a large number of other conventions, declarations and resolutions, which also apply to urban development. The most relevant is the *Habitat Agenda*, which forms a basis for national and international housing and urban policy. It was adopted at the Habitat II Conference in 1996 and reaffirmed by the UN General Assembly in 2001 (Box 22, p 147).

With regard to environmental issues, the Rio Declaration with Agenda 21 was followed up 10 years later in Johannesburg (2002). The outcome was the *Johannesburg Declaration and Plan of Implementation*. The Commission on Sustainable Development (CSD) is in charge of monitoring progress and formulating advice on action. CSD will examine critical areas in a series of 'cycles'. Some of them are very relevant in this context, like water and sanitation and human settlements (2004-2005), energy, transports etc.

The Monterrey consensus on finance for development (2002) stressed the importance of mobilising local financing .

Particularly important for development cooperation is the *Paris Declaration on Aid Effectiveness, Ownership, Harmonization, Alignment, Results and Mutual Accountability* adopted in 2005 by 35 bilateral donors, 26 multilateral organizations, 56 recipient countries and 14 NGOs. Together with the *national poverty reduction strategies* (PRSP) it will guide cooperation strategies and practise during the coming years. The consequences for urban development cooperation are discussed below.

Changing paradigms in development cooperation

Policies and strategies for development cooperation are changing rapidly. Some current trends are contained already in the full title of the 'Paris Declaration'. Another trend is the sharper focus on poverty reduction and that the Millennium Development Goals have taken the lead in setting the agenda.

A general trend has been the noticeable change with respect to level and

Educational, technical and cultural development are features of urban society.
© Johan Wingborg

In September 2000 the heads of state at the UN General Assembly adopted the *Millennium Declaration*. The decisions which were related to development, poverty eradication, environment, HIV/AIDS, financing, trade and development cooperation were later brought together into eight *Millennium Development Goals* (MDGs):

1. Eradicate extreme poverty and hunger
2. Achieve universal primary education
3. Promote gender equality and empower women
4. Reduce child mortality
5. Improve maternal health
6. Combat HIV/AIDS, malaria and other diseases
7. Ensure environmental sustainability
8. Develop a global partnership for development.

The goals are divided into 18 targets with a total of 48 indicators, which are measurable results to be reached by the year 2015 in most cases. Target 11 of Goal 7 calls for, by 2020, a significant improvement in the lives of at least 100 million slum dwellers. It is worth noting that this goal is also stated in the Millennium Declaration itself.

Target 10 of the same goal is to reduce by half, by 2015, the proportion of people without sustainable access to safe drinking water and basic sanitation. Access to adequate water and sanitation alone would have a major health effect. Safe drinking water and basic sanitation are also crucial for achieving the additional goals of reducing child mortality (Goal 4) and important for improving maternal health (Goal 5).

All eight goals are in fact relevant for urban poverty reduction and increased support to urban development would contribute to reaching the goals.

nature of intervention from 'micro to macro', from concrete action to structural reform and a gradual shift from projects and programmes to sector support, and even further to general budget support. According to the Paris Declaration, donors shall align their support to the countries' national strategies. As a consequence there is more interest in national policy reforms. The donor community has insisted on macro-economic reforms since the days of *structural adjustment,* and national *strategies for sustainable development* and *poverty reduction* are now required. The Sector-Wide Approach process (SWAp) is also linked to national policy issues.

While donors increasingly 'interfere' at policy level they also emphasise national ownership – developing countries 'own their development'. This may seem contradictory. But with ownership comes responsibility, and goals and targets need to be based on mutual undertakings by partner countries and development partners. Donors are quite properly concerned to see evidence of commitment to democracy, good governance and human rights and to see a return, in the form of an impact from development efforts. A further aspect of ownership and responsibility is the realization that development must build on domestic resources. Financial support is relatively insignificant and progress is not sustainable if it depends on a continued flow of external resources.

The trends described above mark a significant change in development cooperation – a new global development agenda. Changes take time and may not be complete, but the course is set and support to urban development must be developed within this framework.

Failure and success of urban policies

There have been major paradigm shifts in housing policy over the past decades.

The period after World War II was characterised by public rental housing programmes and eradication of informal settlements. Subsidies were an important part of housing policies and rents were often regulated. The idea of massive public housing as a solution to the needs of a growing urban population in developing countries was doomed to fail. Prices were unaffordable, corrupt procedures and favouritism flourished, and housing programmes invariably missed the target group. Rent control resulted in poor quality and lack of funds for maintenance. In the late 1960s and early 1970s John Turner's writings became influential. Informal suburbs could be seen as the solution rather than the problem; instead of bulldozing them, improving these poor settlements was the way forward.

The second period from the mid 1970s to the mid 1980s marked a break from previous concepts. The World Bank introduced two models: 'sites and services' focused on new development with classic projects in Botswana, El Salvador, Senegal and Tanzania; and 'upgrading' of existing settlements through improved infrastructure – for example in Indonesia, Burkina Faso and Zambia. Both these models were based on the concept of self-help. Housing finance at the time was focused on low-interest loans and subsidies to make housing and services affordable to low-income groups. These were recommendations from the first Habitat Conference in Vancouver in 1976, but the sources of funding and the implications of underpriced services were not discussed.

Other trends during this period were the 'intermediate technology' concept, a growing interest in 'bottom-up' approaches and the first recognition of the role of the informal sector.

The World Bank projects incorporated many good ideas. There was, for the first time, a serious attempt to find solutions to fit the urban problems of developing countries. The projects were intended to demonstrate a replicable model for low-cost housing on a large scale. They were, however, subsidized in several ways. This could be justified for a demonstration project but the transition to full cost recovery was difficult.

The 'top-down' design and a 'bypass' implementation structure meant that communities felt no ownership and were reluctant to pay for improved services. The local authorities provided public land at subsidized prices, but were then not involved in the planning, financing and implementation. In reality there was no institutional capacity for the intended replication.

Several of the projects did have a major impact, such as the slum upgrading programmes in Tunisia and Indonesia. In Amman, Jordan, for example, upgrading involved many interventions and significant improvements in infant and child mortality were observed. But too often the projects were not replicated and the result was isolated enclaves for those lucky households initially selected.

Lessons learned from the previous public housing policy and the following project-based approach contributed to the emergence of the 'enabling approach' of mid 1980s. The International Year of Shelter for the Homeless in 1987 was a starting point for the formulation of this new paradigm, which was articulated in the Global Strategy for Shelter to the Year 2000 (GSS), which was adopted by the UN General Assembly in 1990.

The approach counts on participation from a wide range of actors including NGOs and community-based organizations. Housing and urban development is seen as a multi-sector issue. The task of the state is to create the legal, institutional and economic framework, but not to provide the housing. It is important to stress that the new paradigm retained some of the successful approaches of the 1970s, notably the slum upgrading approach.

The World Bank shifted during this period from project-oriented lending to lending for housing finance. This was also the period of 'Structural Adjustment Programmes (SAP)' addressing macro-economic issues. For the urban poor the SAP brought hardly any benefits. Investment in infrastructure and services declined, poor municipalities became even poorer, formal employment rates went down and the number of poor people increased. It remains to be verified, but it is probable that external support for housing and urban infrastructure to the poorest countries also declined during the 1990s. The financial sector loans from the World Bank tended to reach countries that were less poor than those assisted during the previous phase. Private investments increased dramatically, but the urban sector in the poorest countries did not benefit.

The Habitat II Conference in Istanbul in 1996 adopted The Habitat Agenda, a comprehensive policy framework for urban development integrating the main elements of the previous shelter strategy. Governance, stakeholder involvement, urban management, secure tenure and the envir-

The Habitat Agenda was adopted by 171 governments at the Habitat II Conference in Istanbul 1996, and was reaffirmed by the UN General Assembly in 2001. The Agenda is about sustainable human settlements in an urbanizing world. It has three parts: Goals and Principles, Commitments and Global Plan of Action. The commitments cover:
- adequate shelter for all
- sustainable human settlements
- enablement and participation
- gender equality
- financing
- international cooperation

The main part is the Plan of Action with one section on shelter an one on sustainable urban development. A third section deals with governance and institutional development. International cooperation and the implementation of the agenda are the two final topics.

The Habitat Agenda is by no means a 'building agenda'. Poverty and social aspects, environmental sustainability, urban economy, governance and community participation are salient issues beside more 'technical' matters like shelter delivery systems, land use, energy, transport, cultural heritage and disaster prevention.

onment became more salient issues than before and the role of local governments was emphasised.

Looking back at the second half of the 20th century, it obvious that the understanding of the issues has improved and better informed policies have been formulated at the international level and also in many countries. Unfortunately, this progress has not been accompanied by commensurate support from donors.

Ultimately towns and cities in the developing countries should become equitable and sustainable urban societies spearheading economic, social and cultural development for the benefit of urban as well as rural populations.

Objective and approaches

Objective for urban development cooperation

Sustainable global development cannot be achieved in a world where poverty and inequality persist. In the case of Sweden, the goal for development cooperation is:

> – *to contribute to an environment supportive of poor people's own efforts to improve their quality of life.*

This means that the urban poor shall have improved opportunities for earning a living, for better housing and basic services, for access to health-care and education, but also for better security, for respect for rights and for democracy, for having a voice and the right to be heard.

Development cooperation must contribute to the abolition of urban poverty and even to poverty prevention. This requires development cooperation directly targeted to improve the conditions of the urban poor, but the goal should also be pursued:

> – *through strengthened democratic urban governance.*

This means support for decentralization and local self-governance, but also for good governance and improved urban management at national and local levels based on pro-poor policies.

> – *through facilitating urban contributions to economic growth.*

Economic development is a condition for poverty elimination; economic growth in urban areas is critical for development as a whole, benefiting the rural as well as the urban populations.

> – *through reduction of the environmental burden caused by urban activities.*

This means a better urban environment to benefit public health, especially for the poor, but also reduced pollution of air and water, and less depletion of natural resources, which have an impact at regional and global levels as well.

– through promotion of urban culture including cultural heritage management.

Culture is an important dimension of sustainable development. Lack of access to culture and media, as well as lack of recognition of the culture and the cultural heritage belonging to the poor, are salient aspects of poverty.

Perspectives and approaches

The poor themselves know best what their priorities are. Their voices must be listened to and their rights must be respected.

Good urban governance as well as development support should be based on a rights perspective, which encompasses human rights and democracy, the rule of law and democratic and participatory governance. In the urban context there are, as described earlier, issues where the rights perspective is particularly appropriate. The *rights of everyone to a standard of living adequate for their health and well-being of himself and his family including food, medical care, housing and the necessary social services* are stated in the Universal Declaration on Human Rights. These rights do not mean that states are obliged to provide everyone with free housing. What it means is that states have the responsibility to set up the legal, social and economic environment which will allow households a reasonable chance to satisfy these basic needs. States do have the obligation to protect their citizens against violations of these rights. Forced eviction is a pertinent example of such violation. There are of course circumstances when relocation of people is necessary. But people shall not be victims of arbitrary and ill-informed actions and must always be offered adequate alternatives acceptable to them.

The *rights perspective* applies to security of tenure of land and home, to the legalisation of settlements and livelihood, to the provision of adequate education, and to health and basic services. The rights must encompass all citizens and vulnerable groups – such as children, the aged and the disabled – need particular attention.

The rights perspective does not imply that people should expect governments to solve all their problems. If people and community organizations, for this reason, refrain from making own efforts, it would jeopardise all enabling strategies. A rigid interpretation of the rights approach might thus be counterproductive.

The other perspective, which should permeate urban governance and donor interventions to eliminate urban poverty, is *the perspective of the poor*. What this means is that policies and interventions directed to improve conditions of the poor must be developed on the basis of the priorities that the

urban poor themselves express. This implies that good intentions and 'pro-poor policies' may not suffice. Without the poor themselves being involved, it is not possible to have full information on their conditions and appreciate their real priorities.

Gender equality is a rights issue and a 'crosscutting' theme, which should be 'mainstreamed' – that is to say, applied to every case and every intervention. Most issues related to housing, the informal economy, safety, health and HIV/AIDS are core concerns for women. They are of course crucial for all, but need to be understood from a gender perspective, and then appropriately addressed.

The other important crosscutting theme is *environmental concern*. This study includes sections on urban environmental issues which need particular attention, but environmental aspects should also be mainstreamed. Environmental impacts shall be taken into account and assessed for every programme or project.

Urban contrasts are urban reality: high and low; rich and poor, hope and despair. Mumbai, with more than 18 million people, will soon be the second largest city in the world. Tokyo, twice as big, is still number one.

© Thomas Melin

Strategic reforms of policies and regulatory frameworks would fail if not implemented at the local level. Concerted efforts from donors are needed, but budget support and sector-wide approaches are not sufficient.

Strategic focus

Urban issues and national policies

Most developing countries do not have an urban development and slum upgrading policy. It is assumed that the issues are covered in sector policies for education, health, water, transport, environment and so on. This is only partly true. There may be policies and legislation on local authorities, land and town planning or housing that address urban issues, but overall there is really little consideration for the specific conditions of urban areas. This is also reflected in the structure of the government and the budget: there is rarely a ministry or a budget for urban development. As a consequence there is no focal point, no comprehensive understanding of the situation and no real policy development.

Bilateral and multilateral development cooperation agencies normally deal with the national governments. With no proper counterpart in central government and no representation from local government, it is not surprising that urban issues are not on the agenda.

The situation is unfortunate. It makes it difficult for the government to undertake necessary measures to manage the urban crisis, and it certainly does not contribute to mobilising external support.

There is also a risk that budget support and sector-wide approaches will favour conventional sectors. Urban development could then be left out.

However, we know that the Millennium Development Goals and poverty reduction cannot be achieved without major efforts in the urban areas. It is therefore very important that the situation in urban areas and the conditions of the urban poor are fully appreciated and adequately addressed in the *poverty reduction strategies* now being developed by most developing countries. This is not yet the case; urban poverty is, as a rule, very poorly assessed in the first generation of such strategies (see 'Who are the poor?' p 44).

The poverty reduction strategy offers the opportunity to integrate urban development issues more comprehensively in national policy. The donor community could contribute to this in its support to the process and in its monitoring of the impact.

The context-specific urban conditions also need to be acknowledged and addressed in the sector policies. An example of this need is how education and health services fail to reach the poorest and most vulnerable urban dwellers. Bilateral and multilateral donors in those sectors could play a role in the dialogue and especially when donor consortia negotiate support on a sector-wide scale.

The policy reforms required from the central government to enable a sustainable development of urban centres and eliminate slums are mentioned in 'The key role of central government' (p 86).

Donors need to encourage and give support. UN-HABITAT in particular is in a position to advise on policy matters, but it is the national governments which must realize the need and decide to undertake the necessary reforms.

Reaching impact at the local level

Urban development is, by definition, local. National policies and resource allocation are extremely important, but without action at the local level, cities will not develop and the conditions for the urban poor will not improve. The weakness of the local governments in most developing countries is a major development obstacle. Donor support to policy reforms at the national level will serve no purpose unless they can be implemented. The question is to find ways to reach impact at the local level.

Most important is to strengthen democratic local self-governance. As we have said earlier, central governments should devolve power and financial authority to local governments. Donors already support this process. It has progressed in some countries – particularly in Latin America. The pace of progress is, however, slow. All parties need to intensify their efforts. Local government must be empowered to act, but this is not enough. If they are to take on this wider authority and responsibility, they need not only resources, but also help with institutional development. External assistance is demanded and could play a critical role in creating viable and effective urban governments.

External support to enhance the capability of local government could mean a difference in areas like:
- aspects of good governance
- public administration
- utility reforms
- municipal financing
- environmental management
- local development planning
- land and tenure
- building and planning regulation.

Capacity development of local authorities through training and institutional support is necessary, but civil society institutions also have an important role and supporting them could in combination with formal control mechanisms, like audits, help to prevent corruption and promote good governance. This is not new; donors have supported NGOs and other organizations for a very long time.

Reforms of policies and regulations and strengthened local governance are two fundamental steps in creating an enabling environment for local development.

Concrete actions involving the poor themselves, NGOs and the private sector aiming at improving housing conditions for slum dwellers are also required. The donor community is committed to the Millennium Development Goals, and financial support and technical assistance will be needed. The challenge is to develop effective forms of assistance to local action with an impact that goes beyond that of individual projects. (This is further discussed in 'Tool box', p 157).

To summarize – support through development cooperation will be ineffective if actions at the central level are not linked with support for reaching the local governance and the level of implementation.

Donor harmonization

Urban development is a rather neglected area in international development cooperation. The share of funds allocated is low, the donor agencies are not staffed for the purpose and there is insufficient understanding of the issues. The main actors are multilateral institutions – the World Bank, regional development banks, the EU and of course UN-HABITAT. UN-HABITAT is the leading UN agency, but UNDP, UNEP, WHO and others are all involved with urban issues.

Among the bilateral donors, UK (DFID), USA (USAID), Germany (GTZ and KfW), France (AFD) and Japan (JICA) are most prominent (see also Milbert, 1999). Sweden (Sida) has been an active partner over the past twenty years, with a growing portfolio of bilateral urban and housing projects. There are several examples of collaboration between donors, particularly in programmes in the multilateral sphere. Sweden is an active partner in this collaboration, contributing to the development of common policy positions. With respect to donor harmonization it is an advantage that there is considerable consensus within the donor community on urban policy issues as expressed in the Habitat Agenda.

At country level, the scope for donor harmonization in favour of urban development is often limited because few donors in the country are active in the field. With a strong donor emphasis on harmonization and a donor preference for involvement in those areas where harmonization is feasible, there is then a risk that assistance to urban development could be played down even more. Should this happen, the chance of reaching target 11 of the MDG would decrease instead of increase.

There would be less risk of this happening if future poverty reduction strategies were properly defined and took serious account of the particular needs of the urban poor. Donor consortia supporting the implementation of these strategies could then effectively contribute to eliminating urban slums.

On the global level a promising initiative to reach the MDGs in urban development is the establishment of *Cities Alliance* (CA). This is a network of major multilateral and bilateral donors and other partners. Brazil and South Africa joined in 2004 and 2005 as the first developing countries. The international unions of local authorities were members from the beginning. The objective is to improve the impact and efficiency of urban development cooperation in two key areas: City Development Strategies (CDS) and slum upgrading. During 2000-2004 nearly 50 million USD were invested under this umbrella.

In 2004 the former separate international unions of local authorities (IULA, FMCU-UTO and WACLAC) formed the *United Cities and Local Governments* (UCLG). This is a milestone because all local governments all over the world now have a representative voice. UCLG could play an important role in promoting urban development cooperation in the future.

Harmonized bilateral cooperation means that individual projects would be less frequent and that broader development efforts in consortia with other donors would be the rule. In this context the challenge to reach and empower the urban poor and strengthen weak local authorities calls for new models of cooperation.

Key areas

There is no key that fits all locks. Donors should develop capacity to deal with processes and complexity rather than single-sector approaches.

The ambition of this book has been to present and discuss the most important issues of urban development with a focus on poverty reduction. Most issues are interrelated and the solution of a problem in one area depends on what is happening in another. This is not unique for urban development, although the spatial concentration tends to increase complexity and interrelationships. Realities of course differ from country to country and from city to city.

As a consequence, it is not possible to state as a general rule that one aspect is more important than another. While a donor cannot be expected

to address all problems, priorities should not be expressed only in terms of sectors or subject areas. Previous sections of this book gave examples of other types of priorities: the inclusion of urban aspects in sector-wide programmes; the need for better poverty strategies; the empowerment of local authorities – and so forth.

It should also be recognized that the 'market' for development cooperation is dynamic. Opportunities to have a real effect need to be seized when they appear.

For all these reasons it is not advisable to suggest a very limited set of priority areas here. Broader thematic fields would be a more useful guide to urban development cooperation in general. Within that framework it should then be possible to define – together with local partners and based on local conditions – both the priorities and contents of programmes and projects. Information on the nature of urban challenges in the first three chapters and more detailed suggestions on how the challenges could be met in chapter four should be useful.

The broader priority fields are identified in 'Objective and approaches' (p 148). 'Key areas in pro-poor urban development' (p 136) is an overview of areas where action is required and where assistance through international cooperation could contribute.

In summary, development cooperation should contribute to attaining the MDGs through support to equitable and sustainable urban development and in particular through support to improved urban governance and slum upgrading.

Tool box

The repertory of development cooperation is varied. Ways in which different modalities and instruments can be employed in support to urban development are outlined below. It is not a comprehensive overview; the focus is on bilateral cooperation.

Support can be classified as *financial* ('hardware') or *capacity building* ('software') or as a combination. Financial support could be loans, guarantees, grants or in certain cases, equity contributions. Most support to institutional development, training and other forms of capacity building are donated.

Although poverty is the problem, money is not necessarily the solution. Improved governance and enhanced management capacity are crucial, and sustainable improvement of urban conditions must primarily be based on domestic and local resources. However, in the least developed countries, the badly needed upgrading and expansion of obsolete infrastructure systems to keep pace with urban growth cannot happen without financial sup-

Protests against the government in La Paz, May 2005. The city is the arena where most political opinions and conflicts reach open air. Revolution as well as repression takes place in cities, especially in the capitals, where power resides.

© Jose Luis Quintana / Reuters-Scanpix

In Costa Rica Sida financed a self-help housing programme for squatters between 1988 and 1995. The programme was implemented by a foundation, FUPROVI (Fundacion Promotora de Vivienda) and the development of the foundation into a sustainable institution was a component of the programme. Sida established a revolving fund that was used to give bridging loans for new housing projects and home improvements. The programme was designed as a complement to the national housing policy and aimed at facilitating access for the poor to the national housing finance system. Most loans were replaced by subsidies and credits from this system after a certain time and the money was then used for new projects. An important component was the legalisation of land tenure, which was a condition for obtaining the subsidy.

The methodology of organized self-help building was used from the beginning and was also further developed by FUPROVI. Efficiency and quality was remarkable. Around 1000 families were reached annually. FUPROVI has even developed into a regional training institution in the field of low-income housing and related topics.

Ten years after the Swedish support ended FUPROVI has developed further, the revolving fund has grown considerably, and FUPROVI has become an important actor in housing development in Costa Rica.

port. Also the need to develop new opportunities for housing and municipal financing would be substantially facilitated with external capital, although such support must be designed to avoid negative effects on the local financial market.

Another form of donor intervention is through *dialogue*. As mentioned earlier, dialogue does give an important opportunity to put urban issues on the agenda. Donors should, for instance, insist that poverty reduction strategies should address urban poverty adequately. The same applies to many forms of budget support and sector support programmes. These modalities are expected to increase and it is important that urban issues are included. However, for reasons explained earlier, it is unlikely that the slum target of the MDGs could be reached without specially targeted programmes and projects as well.

Although aiming at local impacts, a first priority is urban programmes with a national coverage. Support to policy reforms and their implementation is one example. Support to training of municipal personnel, municipal auditing, urban research, etc are others. In most countries there are associations of local authorities which could play an important role to improve municipal governance.

Financial support to housing and municipal finance should be nationwide. Channelling through the government is an option, but market-based solutions – which also serve to develop the financial sector – are preferable. Special development funds could be established with loans or grants from donors, but guarantee instruments could also be useful. Support to the micro-finance sector is particularly important for poverty reduction. As mentioned before, such support must be carefully designed to prevent unhealthy subsidies and market distortions. However, housing micro-finance is still in an early stage of development and both seed money and other forms of support are justified.

Civil society has a key role to play and supporting relevant organizations is essential to reach the goals. NGOs that operate effectively on a national scale exist in some countries. Appropriate support may enable other NGOs to extend their range. Support through associations of NGOs may be a means of reaching major impact.

The nation-wide approach is a logical response to the need to reach scale, but support at city level should not be excluded, particularly since many issues can be addressed only at the local level. If resources admit, city level interventions could be parallel or repeated over time and thus reach many urban centres.

A good example of city-specific support is 'City Development Strategies (CDS)' (Box 13, p 97). They are, in a sense, the poverty reduction strategies at local level and provide an opportunity for donors to contribute to local development based on local priorities. Although the CDS are not based on the concept of externally financed development, it is evident that such support would be extremely helpful. The credibility of participatory processes is also strengthened if the consultation process is, within a reasonable time, followed by concrete action.

A model with many advantages is for a donor to enter into *long-term cooperation with one or more selected cities*. The contents of the cooperation would be agreed upon at regular intervals and may shift focus over time, according to local needs and priorities. Ideally, this form of cooperation shall be coordinated with other donors entering into similar partnerships with other cities.

A variety is the *twinning* between cities in developed and developing countries. This should not be confused with the ordinary social and cultural relations that many municipalities have established with towns in other parts of the world. Twinning here means a formal agreement which specifies the areas of cooperation and the particular objectives. The idea is that the developing country city is given the opportunity to learn from the experience and know-how of the developed country city. The activities are financed by the donor agency.

A project approach at city level may also be needed for support to infrastructure investments, utility reforms, physical planning or slum upgrading. Pilot projects to test new approaches may be justified. However, single projects should be an exception and city-wide or nation-wide programmes the rule. The magnitude of the challenge – to improve the living conditions of the many millions of urban poor and prevent the formation of new slums – calls for action on a commensurate scale. A significant scale of operation can be reached in more than one way, however. Effects over time need to be taken into account. An activity that at first is limited in scale, but designed to grow and go on for a long time may finally have greater effect than a major one-time project. Scale is important but sustainability and replicability are as important.

Many think that the costs for slum upgrading are astronomic. However, less than USD 20 billion is required annually to reach MDG target 11 and also prevent the formation of new slums. This represents 10 per cent of current aggregate investments in housing. Claims on ODA would be USD 5.5 billion, which is 8 per cent of total ODA for 2003.

Funding needs

Total needs and current investments

The MDG target 11 is to improve the conditions of 100 million slum dwellers by 2020. An additional 570 million people would need adequate alternatives if the formation of new slums during the same time period is to be avoided.

In developing countries housing and related infrastructure investments tend to be in the range of 3–8 per cent of GDP, depending largely on the income level of the country concerned. In aggregate, these investments are around USD 100 billion for urban infrastructure (excluding health and education facilities in urban areas) and around USD 200 billion for housing. These investments fall well short of the needs and often do not reach the poor. However, improving the infrastructure in slums in the developing countries would represent only 3 per cent of GDP, according to Cities Alliance.

The total investment for 670 million slum dwellers would, according to the Millennium Project , be close to USD 300 billion (annually 18.5 billion) during the period 2005-2020 and would include: security of tenure, housing improvement, physical infrastructure (water, sanitation, drainage, road, electricity), primary schools and health clinics.[33]

The World Panel on Financing Water Infrastructure (2003) estimates that in order to meet the MDG targets related to water supply and sanitation, annual investments need to double from the present level of USD 30–35 billion. Most of these investments would be made in urban areas and include water and sanitation in slum areas, which is why there is some double counting.

ODA contributions

Multilateral and bilateral assistance for housing and all urban infrastructure appears to be no more than USD 6 billion annually. While private investments in infrastructure facilities increased rapidly during the 1990s, only

---

33) UN Millennium Project, Task Force on Improving the Lives of Slum Dwellers (2005) *A home in the city*, Earthscan, London

about 5 per cent of such investments were devoted to urban water supply and sanitation. This means that donors and outside investors play a marginal role in addressing the urban problems of the developing world. The solutions have to be 'home-grown' and the resources mobilised locally, but catalytic interventions by donors could be effective especially with regard to the poor.

In the poorest countries, even massive efforts by governments, communities, households and private enterprises will not be enough to meet the targets related to slum upgrading, water and sanitation; financial support from development banks and donors is required. The need for increased donor assistance is greatest in Sub-Saharan Africa, given its rapid urban growth, its shortage of financial resources, large slum populations, and severe infrastructure deficiencies.

The Millennium Project Task Force on Improving the Lives of Slum Dwellers expects loans to residents and their own contributions to cover 40 per cent of the investment costs.[34] It is further assumed that local and national governments would cover 30 per cent, leaving roughly USD 5.5 billion annually to be contributed by international donors. This would be 8 per cent of total development cooperation funds. Since current bilateral and multilateral assistance to slum upgrading may amount to less than USD 0.8 billion annually, it is obvious that development assistance to slum upgrading has to increase substantially – perhaps seven times – to make tangible progress towards the MDG target.

Although this estimate is based on actual experience and is adjusted to regional conditions, it is evident that both the total investments and the cost-sharing assumptions are uncertain. The estimate does show, however, that required resources and donor contributions are moderate in a global perspective. To reach the goal does not require a miracle, but it does require political will and international solidarity.

FURTHER READING
Garau P, Sclar E D, Carolini G Y. 2005. *A home in the city*. UN Millennium Project. Task Force on Improving the Lives of Slum Dwellers. Earthscan. London.

34) The Millennium Project is an advisory body commissioned by the UN Secretary General. It has carried out the work in thematic task forces comprising more than 250 experts from around the world.

A final word

National governments and donors have for too long ignored the challenges of rapid urban growth; they have neglected urban poverty, slums and environmental degradation. The result is an urban crisis. Concerted and well targeted efforts are now required. Governments must undertake fundamental policy reforms, and development cooperation must increase and be more effective. A full understanding of these issues – the purpose of this book – is a first step towards the ultimate goal – an urban world without poverty.

ANNEXES

Tables

UN urbanization statistics

The main source of statistical information in this report is the *World Urbanization Prospects: The 2003 Revision*, published by UN in 2004. This publication is revised every second year to include new census results and survey data and The 2003 Revision was current at the time of publication.

The revisions rarely affect long established trends on the global and regional level. On the national level access to new census results often means modifications of estimates and projections.

Table A1. Percentage urban population by major areas and regions

Major area, region, country or area	1960	1975	1990	2005	2020
WORLD	32.9	37.3	43.2	49.2	55.9
More developed regions	58.6	67.2	71.8	74.9	78.7
Less developed regions	21.7	26.9	35.2	43.2	51.4
Least developed countries	9.5	14.7	20.9	27.7	36.5
AFRICA	18.6	25.3	31.9	39.7	47.8
Eastern Africa	7.4	12.4	19.2	27.0	35.2
Middle Africa	17.9	26.7	30.9	37.9	47.6
Northern Africa	30.1	38.6	44.7	50.4	57.6
Southern Africa	41.8	44.1	46.2	54.7	61.9
Western Africa	14.8	22.6	32.7	43.6	53.0
ASIA	19.8	24.0	31.9	39.9	48.5
Eastern Asia	20.3	23.3	33.0	44.5	56.2
South-central Asia	18.2	22.2	27.3	30.7	37.1
South-eastern Asia	18.5	23.4	31.6	43.7	54.5
Western Asia	35.0	48.4	61.2	65.5	69.3
EUROPE	56.7	66.0	71.5	73.3	76.6
LATIN AMERICA AND THE CARIBBEAN	49.3	61.2	71.1	77.6	82.3
Caribbean	40.5	51.0	58.7	64.7	69.6
Central America	46.5	57.2	65.9	69.7	74.2
South America	51.4	64.0	74.5	82.1	86.8
NORTHERN AMERICA	69.9	73.8	75.4	80.8	84.8
OCEANIA	65.9	71.7	70.1	73.3	74.2

Table A2. **Average annual urban growth rates (%) by major areas and regions**

Major area, region and country	1960-1965	1975-1980	1990-1995	2005-2010	2020-2025
WORLD	3.08	2.72	2.35	2.00	1.66
More developed regions	2.12	1.25	0.75	0.50	0.43
Less developed regions	4.15	3.90	3.21	2.57	2.01
Least developed countries	5.36	5.66	4.61	4.22	3.66
AFRICA	4.83	4.46	4.15	3.35	2.84
Eastern Africa	6.04	6.65	5.17	4.07	3.40
Middle Africa	5.60	3.91	4.38	4.19	3.62
Northern Africa	4.64	3.51	2.89	2.59	2.13
Southern Africa	2.99	2.69	3.62	0.70	0.49
Western Africa	5.36	5.53	4.94	3.79	2.98
ASIA	3.84	3.73	3.11	2.50	1.94
Eastern Asia	3.77	3.39	3.08	2.32	1.35
South-central Asia	3.57	4.00	2.82	2.59	2.64
South-eastern Asia	3.94	3.97	4.01	2.95	1.94
Western Asia	5.30	4.07	2.95	2.31	1.94
EUROPE	2.05	1.26	0.34	0.10	0.11
LATIN AMERICA AND THE CARIBBEAN	4.32	3.47	2.33	1.70	1.12
Caribbean	3.71	2.73	2.04	1.24	0.97
Central America	4.63	3.75	2.35	1.86	1.38
South America	4.29	3.46	2.35	1.69	1.04
NORTHERN AMERICA	2.04	1.04	1.58	1.31	1.01
OCEANIA	2.83	0.98	1.97	1.18	0.91

Table A3. **Urban population by major areas and regions (thousands of inhabitants)**

Major area, region, country or area	1960	1975	1990	2005	2020
WORLD	992,753	1,516,326	2,273,241	3,171,990	4,215,397
More developed regions	536,185	703,624	825,245	905,558	974,228
Less developed regions	456,569	812,702	1,447,996	2,266,432	3,241,169
Least developed countries	23,498	52,120	107,839	208,375	381,129
AFRICA	51,557	103,204	198,794	352,927	568,199
Eastern Africa	6,110	15,471	37,469	76,340	135,788
Middle Africa	5,716	12,335	21,928	40,252	73,212
Northern Africa	20,248	37,616	63,984	95,977	138,277
Southern Africa	8,265	12,871	19,405	28,441	31,169
Western Africa	11,219	24,912	56,007	111,918	189,752
ASIA	337,572	574,844	1,011,737	1,562,130	2,214,364
Eastern Asia	160,431	255,735	445,086	682,196	921,854
South-central Asia	112,687	195,641	334,311	496,429	739,066
South-eastern Asia	41,140	75,110	138,937	243,765	359,842
Western Asia	23,314	48,358	93,403	139,739	193,602
EUROPE	342,842	445,994	516,223	531,182	540,068
LATIN AMERICA AND THE CARIBBEAN	107,599	197,065	313,879	433,183	542,392
Caribbean	8,264	13,852	19,900	25,478	30,344
Central America	22,985	44,981	73,441	102,401	132,055
South America	76,350	138,232	220,538	305,304	379,992
NORTHERN AMERICA	142,714	179,761	213,889	268,371	321,968
OCEANIA	10,469	15,458	18,720	24,199	28,405

Table A4. Percentage of urban population in selected countries

AFRICA	1960	1975	1990	2005	2020
Algeria	30.4	40.3	51.4	60.0	67.9
Angola	10.4	17.4	26.1	37.2	48.7
Botswana	3.0	12.8	42.3	52.5	60.2
Burkina Faso	4.7	6.3	13.6	18.6	26.1
Burundi	2.2	3.2	6.3	10.6	17.0
Egypt	37.9	43.5	43.4	42.3	47.4
Eritrea	8.7	12.7	15.8	20.8	29.9
Ethiopia	6.4	9.5	12.7	16.2	22.3
Kenya	7.4	12.9	24.7	41.6	55.9
Malawi	4.4	7.7	11.6	17.2	25.1
Mali	11.1	16.2	23.8	33.7	44.6
Morocco	29.2	37.8	48.4	58.8	67.5
Mozambique	3.8	8.7	21.1	38.0	52.8
Namibia	15.0	20.6	26.6	33.5	43.4
Nigeria	15.2	23.4	35.0	48.3	58.9
Rwanda	2.4	4.0	5.3	21.8	48.5
Somalia	17.3	25.5	29.4	35.9	46.4
South Africa	46.6	48.0	48.8	57.9	65.2
United Republic of Tanzania	4.7	10.1	21.7	37.5	50.7
Tunisia	36.0	49.9	57.9	64.4	70.2
Uganda	5.1	8.3	11.2	12.4	15.7
Zambia	18.5	34.8	39.4	36.5	43.5
Zimbabwe	12.6	19.6	29.0	35.9	44.6

LATIN AMERICA AND THE CARIBBEAN	1960	1975	1990	2005	2020
Bolivia	36.8	41.3	55.6	64.4	71.2
Brazil	44.9	61.2	74.7	84.2	89.7
Chile	67.8	78.4	83.3	87.7	91.1
Colombia	49.1	60.0	68.7	77.4	82.8
Costa Rica	34.3	42.5	53.6	61.7	69.3
Cuba	54.9	64.2	73.6	76.0	79.4
El Salvador	38.3	41.5	49.2	60.1	66.5
Guatemala	31.1	36.7	41.1	47.2	54.6
Haiti	15.6	21.7	29.5	38.8	49.0
Honduras	22.7	32.1	40.3	46.4	54.0
Mexico	50.8	62.8	72.5	76.0	80.2
Nicaragua	39.6	48.9	53.1	58.1	65.5
Paraguay	35.6	39.0	48.7	58.5	67.0
Peru	46.8	61.5	68.9	74.6	79.6

ASIA	1960	1975	1990	2005	2020
Afghanistan	8.0	13.3	18.2	24.3	34.1
Armenia	51.2	63.0	66.9	64.1	65.2
Azerbaijan	48.1	51.5	53.7	49.9	53.5
Bangladesh	5.1	9.9	19.8	25.0	32.4
Cambodia	10.3	10.3	12.6	19.7	29.6
China	16.0	17.4	27.4	40.5	53.6
Democratic Republic of Timor-Leste	10.3	8.9	7.8	7.8	11.2
Georgia	43.0	49.5	55.1	51.5	53.0
India	18.0	21.3	25.5	28.7	34.7
Indonesia	14.6	19.3	30.6	47.9	61.6
Iraq	42.9	61.4	69.7	66.8	67.7
Jordan	50.9	57.8	72.2	79.3	82.2
Kazakhstan	44.6	52.2	57.0	55.9	60.3
Kyrgyzstan	34.2	37.9	37.7	33.7	37.7
Lao People's Dem. Republic	7.9	11.1	15.4	21.6	30.8
Lebanon	39.6	67.0	83.2	88.0	90.8
Mongolia	35.7	48.7	57.0	57.0	61.7
Nepal	3.1	5.0	8.9	15.8	23.2
Occupied Palestinian Terr.	44.0	59.6	66.0	71.9	77.3
Philippines	30.3	35.6	48.8	62.6	71.8
Sri Lanka	17.9	22.0	21.3	21.0	24.2
Tajikistan	33.2	35.5	31.6	24.2	26.2
Thailand	19.7	23.8	29.4	32.5	39.7
Viet Nam	14.7	18.9	20.3	26.7	35.8

EUROPE	1960	1975	1990	2005	2020
Albania	30.6	32.7	36.1	45.0	54.4
Belarus	32.3	50.3	66.1	71.6	76.9
Bosnia and Herzegovina	19.0	31.3	39.2	45.3	54.4
Croatia	30.2	45.1	54.0	59.9	67.2
Republic of Moldova	23.4	35.8	46.9	46.3	53.2
Russian Federation	53.7	66.4	73.4	73.3	75.3
Serbia and Montenegro	28.6	43.0	50.9	52.3	58.0
TFYR Macedonia	34.0	50.6	57.8	59.7	64.0

Table A5. Average annual urban growth rates (%) for selected countries

AFRICA	1960-1965	1975-1980	1990-1995	2005-2010	2020-2025
Algeria	6.22	4.67	3.26	2.45	1.64
Angola	5.07	5.44	5.54	4.92	4.09
Botswana	7.71	10.78	5.07	0.54	0.27
Burkina Faso	3.81	8.02	5.11	5.18	5.13
Burundi	2.56	8.28	5.05	6.57	5.06
Egypt	3.95	2.39	1.70	2.39	2.62
Eritrea	6.12	4.19	2.23	5.63	4.25
Ethiopia	5.69	3.50	5.03	4.27	4.60
Kenya	6.20	8.16	6.88	3.67	1.92
Malawi	4.55	6.73	3.83	4.42	4.28
Mali	4.96	4.86	5.13	5.20	4.56
Morocco	4.45	4.01	3.21	2.56	1.76
Mozambique	6.33	10.85	7.74	4.22	2.42
Namibia	4.62	3.99	4.55	2.54	2.29
Nigeria	5.49	5.94	5.35	3.72	2.67
Rwanda	4.93	6.40	3.00	9.30	3.93
Somalia	5.21	9.98	1.68	5.40	4.69
South Africa	2.88	2.50	3.59	0.65	0.40
Tunisia	3.69	3.31	2.87	1.59	1.31
Uganda	8.11	3.98	3.94	4.67	5.67
United Republic of Tanzania	5.08	10.67	7.66	4.24	2.87
Zambia	8.04	5.98	1.55	2.32	2.59
Zimbabwe	6.20	5.83	4.06	1.48	1.38

ASIA	1960-1965	1975-1980	1990-1995	2005-2010	2020-2025
Afghanistan	5.42	4.31	8.35	5.92	4.40
Armenia	4.88	2.67	-1.57	-0.43	0.09
Azerbaijan	3.59	2.10	1.00	1.15	1.79
Bangladesh	6.25	10.70	4.08	3.45	3.20
Cambodia	3.48	2.25	5.62	5.18	3.92
China	3.93	3.90	3.78	2.79	1.54
Democratic Republic of Timor-Leste	0.59	-3.78	1.65	4.22	4.15
Georgia	2.48	1.49	-0.84	-0.88	0.11
India	3.18	3.66	2.73	2.38	2.53
Indonesia	3.69	4.90	4.61	3.22	1.67
Iraq	6.37	4.55	2.80	2.52	2.32
Jordan	5.50	3.58	6.94	2.30	1.71
Kazakhstan	4.74	1.79	-0.51	-0.03	0.84

ASIA	1960-1965	1975-1980	1990-1995	2005-2010	2020-2025
Kyrgyzstan	4.32	2.10	-0.16	1.45	2.52
Lao People's Dem. Republic	3.14	3.38	4.70	4.50	3.84
Lebanon	7.40	1.18	3.43	1.49	0.85
Mongolia	5.95	4.14	1.45	1.74	1.73
Nepal	4.27	7.53	6.49	4.64	4.03
Occupied Palestinian Terr.	3.79	3.97	4.63	3.84	3.02
Philippines	3.93	3.75	4.30	2.70	1.72
Sri Lanka	4.58	1.08	1.01	1.13	2.22
Tajikistan	4.92	2.05	-0.41	0.82	3.33
Thailand	3.75	4.71	1.80	1.99	2.26
Viet Nam	4.70	2.56	3.79	3.21	2.85

EUROPE	1960-1965	1975-1980	1990-1995	2005-2010	2020-2025
Albania	3.40	2.73	0.89	2.03	1.58
Belarus	4.18	2.93	0.54	0.09	-0.13
Bosnia and Herzegovina	4.94	3.42	-3.78	1.45	0.85
Croatia	3.34	2.60	-1.04	0.50	0.25
Republic of Moldova	5.29	3.04	-0.44	0.47	0.83
Russian Federation	2.70	1.63	-0.03	-0.49	-0.37
Serbia and Montenegro	4.17	2.43	0.96	0.47	0.73
TFYR Macedonia	4.66	2.49	1.22	0.73	0.90

LATIN AMERICA & THE CARIBBEAN	1960-1965	1975-1980	1990-1995	2005-2010	2020-2025
Bolivia	3.03	4.27	3.63	2.50	1.94
Brazil	5.24	3.95	2.33	1.63	0.83
Chile	3.49	2.23	1.89	1.43	0.96
Colombia	4.42	3.13	2.89	1.96	1.32
Costa Rica	4.30	4.68	3.40	2.49	1.69
Cuba	3.05	2.02	0.87	0.44	0.25
El Salvador	3.40	3.34	3.91	1.92	1.73
Guatemala	4.60	2.87	3.57	3.27	2.77
Haiti	4.09	3.84	3.60	2.95	2.29
Honduras	5.84	5.01	3.91	2.99	2.40
Mexico	4.69	3.79	2.08	1.62	1.08
Nicaragua	4.74	3.68	3.44	2.91	2.38
Paraguay	2.81	4.50	4.06	3.25	2.45
Peru	4.93	3.66	2.39	1.86	1.38

Table A6. **Urban population in selected countries (thousands)**

Major area, region, country or area	1960	1975	1990	2005	2020
AFRICA					
Algeria	3,287	6,460	12,859	19,710	27,468
Angola	503	1,074	2,441	5,409	10,723
Botswana	16	106	573	946	1,002
Burkina Faso	210	387	1,210	2,561	5,592
Burundi	65	118	352	777	1,881
Egypt	10,541	17,082	24,219	31,649	45,916
Eritrea	123	266	490	928	1,969
Ethiopia	1,462	3,141	6,215	11,987	23,353
Kenya	610	1,753	5,823	13,677	21,533
Malawi	155	402	1,101	2,157	4,188
Mali	489	1,020	2,155	4,655	9,880
Morocco	3,397	6,547	11,887	18,547	26,129
Mozambique	287	921	2,842	7,399	12,683
Namibia	94	190	375	681	988
Nigeria	5,690	12,843	30,142	62,904	104,339
Rwanda	69	176	361	1,874	5,606
Somalia	488	1,054	2,106	3,861	8,314
South Africa	8,113	12,379	17,994	26,228	28,476
Tunisia	1,521	2,825	4,755	6,465	8,156
Uganda	346	899	1,937	3,432	7,329
United Republic of Tanzania	481	1,630	5,657	14,387	25,225
Zambia	581	1,765	3,231	4,031	5,902
Zimbabwe	469	1,202	3,034	4,650	5,785
ASIA					
Afghanistan	803	1,907	2,517	6,311	13,674
Armenia	956	1,779	2,372	1,950	1,908
Azerbaijan	1,872	2,930	3,864	4,253	5,280
Bangladesh	2,663	7,410	21,627	38,128	63,224
Cambodia	559	731	1,228	2,927	5,981
China	105,245	161,439	316,554	535,983	765,597
Democratic Republic of Timor-Leste	52	60	58	67	127
Georgia	1,790	2,432	3,006	2,587	2,428
India	79,414	132,271	216,133	315,276	455,823
Indonesia	13,993	25,971	55,699	107,880	160,775
Iraq	2,937	6,764	12,090	17,750	25,714
Jordan	456	1,120	2,350	4,562	6,216
Kazakhstan	4,461	7,374	9,586	8,594	9,297

Major area, region, country or area	1960	1975	1990	2005	2020
ASIA					
Kyrgyzstan	742	1,250	1,657	1,781	2,349
Lao People's Dem. Republic	173	335	638	1,280	2,451
Lebanon	735	1,854	2,256	3,310	3,991
Mongolia	342	704	1,264	1,520	1,988
Nepal	311	669	1,667	4,166	8,082
Occupied Palestinian Terr.	485	748	1,422	2,743	4,686
Philippines	8,197	14,942	29,804	51,819	73,763
Sri Lanka	1,738	2,971	3,585	4,073	5,118
Tajikistan	691	1,223	1,675	1,538	2,032
Thailand	5,233	9,811	16,003	20,820	28,569
Viet Nam	4,946	9,061	13,383	22,335	35,809
EUROPE					
Albania	493	785	1,188	1,448	1,929
Belarus	2,649	4,714	6,782	7,025	7,082
Bosnia and Herzegovina	605	1,172	1,691	1,908	2,315
Croatia	1,220	1,924	2,617	2,637	2,815
Republic of Moldova	703	1,376	2,047	1,972	2,216
Russian Federation	64,406	89,167	108,830	103,730	97,201
Serbia and Montenegro	2,299	3,905	5,166	5,503	6,003
TFYR Macedonia	474	847	1,103	1,239	1,398
LATIN AMERICA AND THE CARIBBEAN					
Bolivia	1,232	1,966	3,706	5,881	8,311
Brazil	32,693	66,119	111,171	154,002	188,143
Chile	5,161	8,102	10,908	14,190	17,193
Colombia	8,283	15,227	24,028	35,293	45,774
Costa Rica	457	871	1,649	2,670	3,698
Cuba	3,832	5,977	7,827	8,627	9,165
El Salvador	989	1,710	2,516	4,034	5,325
Guatemala	1,233	2,210	3,597	6,120	9,742
Haiti	592	1,066	2,038	3,314	4,997
Honduras	431	968	1,960	3,370	5,108
Mexico	18,751	37,090	60,304	80,881	100,375
Nicaragua	610	1,220	2,029	3,328	5,031
Paraguay	655	1,036	2,054	3,603	5,642
Peru	4,649	9,318	14,988	20,864	26,971

Table A7. The largest urban agglomerations in selected countries, 2005

Country	Urban agglomeration	Population (thousands)	As per cent of urban pop.
AFRICA			
Algeria	Algiers	3,260	16.5
Angola	Luanda	2,839	52.5
Botswana	Gaborone	199	
Burkina Faso	Ouagadougou	870	34.0
Burundi	Bujumbura	378	
Egypt	Cairo	11,146	35.2
Eritrea	Asmara	556	
Ethiopia	Addis Ababa	2,899	24.2
Kenya	Nairobi	2,818	20.6
Malawi	Lilongwe	587	
Mali	Bamako	1,379	29.6
Morocco	Casablanca	3,743	20.2
Mozambique	Maputo	1,316	17.8
Namibia	Windhoek	237	
Nigeria	Lagos	11,135	17.7
Rwanda	Kigali	656	
Somalia	Mogadishu	1,257	32.6
South Africa	Johannesburg	3,288	12.5
Tunisia	Tunis	2,063	31.9
Uganda	Kampala	1,345	39.2
United Republic of Tanzania	Dar es Salaam	2,683	18.6
Zambia	Lusaka	1,450	36.0
Zimbabwe	Harare	1,527	32.9
ASIA			
Afghanistan	Kabul	3,288	52.1
Armenia	Yerevan	1,066	54.7
Azerbaijan	Baku	1,830	43.0
Bangladesh	Dhaka	12,560	32.9
Cambodia	Phnom Penh	1,174	40.1
China	Beijing	10,849	2.0
China	Shanghai	12,665	2.4
Democratic Republic of Timor-Lester	Dili	49	
Georgia	Tbilisi	1,042	40.3
India	Calcutta	14,299	4.5
India	Delhi	15,334	4.9
India	Mumbai (Bombay)	18,336	5.8
Indonesia	Jakarta	13,194	12.2
Iraq	Baghdad	5,910	33.3
Jordan	Amman	1,292	28.3

Country	Urban agglomeration	Population (thousands)	As per cent of urban pop.
ASIA			
Kazakhstan	Almaty	1,103	12.8
Kyrgyzstan	Bishkek	828	46.5
Lao People's Dem Republic	Vientiane	716	*
Lebanon	Beirut	1,875	56.7
Mongolia	Ulaanbaatar	842	55.4
Nepal	Kathmandu	741	*
Occupied Palestinian Terr.			
Philippines	Metro Manila	10,677	20.6
Sri Lanka	Colombo	648	*
Tajikistan	Dushanbe	554	*
Thailand	Bangkok	6,604	31.7
Viet Nam	Ho Chi Minh City	5,030	22.5
EUROPE			
Albania	Tirana	367	*
Belarus	Minsk	1,709	24.3
Bosnia and Herzegovina	Sarajevo	579	*
Croatia	Zagreb	688	*
Republic of Moldova	Chisinau	662	*
Russian Federation	Moscow	10,672	10.3
Serbia and Montenegro	Belgrade	1,116	20.3
TFYR Macedonia	Skopje	447	*
LATIN AMERICA			
Bolivia	La Paz	1,533	26.1
Brazil	São Paulo	18,333	11.9
Chile	Santiago	5,623	39.6
Colombia	Santa Fé de Bogotá	7,594	21.5
Costa Rica	San José	1,145	42.9
Cuba	Havana	2,192	25.4
El Salvador	San Salvador	1,472	36.5
Guatemala	Guatemala City	982	16.0
Haiti	Port-au-Prince	2,090	63.1
Honduras	Tegucigalpa	1,061	31.5
Mexico	Mexico City	19,013	23.5
Nicaragua	Managua	1,159	34.8
Paraguay	Asunción	1,750	48.6
Peru	Lima	8,180	39.2

* Population in 2003, not 2005

Table A8. Population of the 15 largest cities (millions)

There were 22 agglomerations with more than 10 million inhabitants in 2003. The
population figures for the three years illustrate the dynamic.

Megacities	1995	2003	2015
Tokyo	33.6	35	36.2
Mexico City	16.8	18.7	20.6
New York-Newark	16.9	18.3	19.7
Sao Paulo	15.9	17.9	20
Mumbai	14.1	17.4	22.6
Delhi	10.1	14.1	20.9
Calcutta	11.9	13.8	16.8
Buenos Aires	11.9	13	14.6
Shanghai	13.1	12.8	12.7
Jakarta	9.2	12.3	17.5
Los Angeles	11.3	12	12.9
Dhaka	8.2	11.6	17.9
Osaka	11.1	11.2	11.4
Rio de Janeiro	10.2	11.2	12.4
Karachi	8.5	11.1	16.2
Beijing	10.8	10.8	11.1
Cairo	9.7	10.8	13.1
Moscow	9.6	10.5	10.9
Metro Manila	9.4	10.4	12.6
Lagos	6.4	10.1	17

Table A9. The 10 largest urban agglomerations 1950–2015

1950	1975	2003	2015
New York	**Tokyo**	**Tokyo**	**Tokyo**
Tokyo	**New York/Newark**	**Mexico City**	**Mumbai**
London	Shanghai	**New York/Newark**	**Delhi**
Paris	Mexico City	**Sao Paulo**	**Mexico City**
Moscow	Osaka	**Mumbai**	**Sao Paulo**
Shanghai	Sao Paulo	Delhi	**New York/Newark**
Rehn-Ruhr	Buenos Aires	Calcutta	**Dhaka**
Buenos Aires	Los Angeles	Buenos Aires	**Jakarta**
Chicago	Paris	Shanghai	**Lagos**
Calcutta	Beijing	Jakarta	**Calcutta**

Cities in bold type have more than 15 million inhabitants

Table A10. **The world's fastest growing cities, 1950–2000**

URBAN CENTRE	COUNTRY	POPULATION (thousands) 1900	1950	2000	Compound growth rate	Annual average increment in pop. 1950–2000 (thousands)
The world's fastest growing large cities 1950–2000 according to annual average increment in population						
Tokyo	Japan	1497	11,275	34,450	2.26	464
Mexico City	Mexico	415	2,883	18,066	3.74	304
Sao Paulo	Brazil	240	2,313	17,099	4.08	296
Mumbai (Bombay)	India	776	2,981	16,086	3.43	262
Delhi	India	209	1,390	12,441	4.48	221
Dhaka	Bangladesh	90	417	10,159	6.59	195
Jakarta	Indonesia	115	1,452	11,018	4.14	191
Karachi	Pakistan	136	1,028	10,032	4.66	180
Seoul	Republic of Korea	201	1,021	9,917	4.65	178
Calcutta, Kolkata	India	1085	4,446	13,058	2.18	172
The world's fastest growing large cities 1950–2000 according to population growth rates						
Karaj	Iran (Islamic Republic of)		7	1,063	10.57	21
Brasilia	Brazil		36	2,746	9.06	54
Abidjan	Côte D'Ivoire		59	3,057	8.22	60
Lusaka	Zambia		26	1,307	8.15	26
Faridabad	India		22	1,018	7.97	20
Dubai	United Arab Emirates		20	893	7.89	17
Kaduna	Nigeria		28	1,194	7.79	23
Riyadh	Saudi Arabia	30	111	4,519	7.69	88
Las Vegas	USA		35	1,335	7.55	26
Ulsan	Republic of Korea		29	1,011	7.36	20

Table A11. Sub-national governments' share of total government revenues and expenditures

Region or country	Revenue share (%)	Expenditure share (%)	Region or country	Revenue share (%)	Expenditure share (%)
Asia			Nicaragua	9.4	8.6
China [1]	51.3	53.9	Paraguay	2.3	2.6
India [1]	33.0	45.2	Peru	6.1	19.9
Indonesia	3.1	10.1	**Middle East & Northern Africa**		
Papua New Guinea	3.2	12.0	Bahrain	2.3	2.8
Philippines	4.7	8.7	Iran, Islamic Republic of	6.0	4.9
Thailand	8.0	8.4	Tunisia	2.2	4.5
Sri Lanka	3.6	3.7	**Sub-Saharan Africa**		
Eastern Europe & Central Asia			Burkina Faso		3.7
Azerbaijan	15.1	21.9	Ethiopia	1.6	1.5
Belarus	36.1	38.8	Kenya	5.4	3.5
Croatia	12.1	11.6	Madagascar	5.7	
Kazakhstan	29.7	32.8	Malawi		5.7
Kyrgyz Republic	17.9	25.5	South Africa	10.2	34.2
Moldova	18.8	20.8	Uganda	5.4	5.7
Slovenia	9.3	11.4	Zambia	5.1	4.2
Tajikistan	27.8	30.9	Zimbabwe	14.8	13.7
Latin America					
Bolivia	21.6	29.3			
Colombia	15.7	27.7			
Ecuador	18.8	18.3			
Guatemala	3.7	4.7			

Note 1: Federal Systems
Comment: The data are from varying years in the late 1990s.
Source: Data derived from IMF's Government Finance Statistics and presented on the World Bank's website for Decentralization & Subnational Regional Economics.

Source: www1.worldbank.org/publicsector/decentralization/indicators.xls

Definitions

Urban means city, town or other settlements where a majority of the population has an income from activity in the urban economy, which means activities other than agriculture, forestry, hunting and fishing (except of course major fishing ports) Sometimes urban is understood as relating to big cities but here the definition includes small towns as well.

Urbanization is a term that suffers from a confusing variety of definitions, or is not defined at all. Among the most common definitions we find the following:

1a. the proportion (per cent) of the total population that lives in urban centres or
1b. the number of people living there;
2a. the growth in the proportion (per cent) of the total population living in urban centres;
2b. the growth in the number of people living there;
3. the social process by which a population adjusts to the urban way of life;
4. the physical spread of built-up land.

Here the word is used mainly with the meaning of 2a and b but also 3 in the sense of urbanization as a transformation process of the society with economic, social and cultural implications.

Urbanization level. In this report we use urbanization level to mean the proportion (per cent) of the total population in a country living in urban centres.

Urban growth. By urban growth we mean the net increment of the urban population.

Urban growth rate. The urban growth rate is annual urban growth as a percentage of the urban population at the end of the previous year.

Urbanization rate or the rate of urbanization is the difference between the rate of growth of a country's total population and the rate of growth of its urban population.

Population growth is the annual net increment of the population when fertility, mortality and migration are all taken into account.

Natural population growth is the excess of birth over deaths. In the text it is also referred to as natural growth.

City and **town** are distinguished by local traditional or administrative definitions that vary among the English-speaking countries. Here the word city is usually used for bigger agglomerations and town for smaller ones.

Acronyms

APHRC African Population and Health Research Centre, Nairobi
CA Cities Alliance
BOT Build Operate Transfer
CBO Community-Based Organization
CDS City Development Strategy
COHRE Centre on Housing Rights and Evictions, Geneva
CSD Commission on Sustainable Development
CGAP Consultative Group to Assist the Poor (donor consortium on micro-finance with secretariat in the WB)
CLIFF Community-Led Infrastructure Finance Facility
CODI Community Organization Development Institute, Thailand (formerly UDCO)
DHS Demographic and Health Surveys
EIA Environmental Impact Assessment
FDLG Fideicomiso para el Desarollo Local en Guatemala
FUPROVI Fundacion Promotora de Vivienda, Costa Rica
GDP Gross Domestic Product
GNI Gross National Income
HDFC Housing Development Finance Corporation, India
HPFP Homeless Peoples' Federation of Philippines
HUDCO Housing and Urban Development Corporation, India
IFI International Finance Institution
IIED International Institute for Environment and Development, London
ILO International Labour Organization
KfW Kreditanstalt für Wiederaufbau
MDGs Millennium Development Goals
MFI Micro-Finance Institution
MHT Mahila Housing Trust
NACHU National Cooperative Housing Union Ltd, Kenya

NGO	Non-Governmental Organization
NURCHA	National Urban Reconstruction and Housing Agency, South Africa
ODA	Official Development Assistance
ODI	Overseas Development Institute, London
OPP	Orangi Pilot Project, Pakistan
PPI	Private Participation in Infrastructure
PPP	Public-Private Partnership
PRODEL	Programa de Desarollo Local, Nicaragua
PRS(P)	Poverty Reduction Strategy (Paper)
SAP	Structural Adjustment Programmes
SEI	Stockholm Environment Institute
SEWA	Self-Employed Women's Association, India
Sida	Swedish International Development Cooperation Agency
SWAp	Sector Wide Approach process
TB	Tuberculosis
UCLG	United Cities and Local Governments
UDCO	Urban Community Development Office, Thailand (now CODI)
UMP	Urban Management Programme
UN	United Nations
UNDP	United Nations Development Programme
UNEP	United Nations Environmental Programme
UNESCO	United Nations Educational Scientific and Cultural Organization
UNICEF	United Nations Children Fund
USD	US dollar
WB	World Bank
WHO	World Health Organization

References

ACCION and CHF International (2002) *The Enabling Environment for Housing Microfinance in Kenya,* Cities Alliance Shelter Finance for the Poor Series, Washington, DC

APHRC (2002) *Population and Health Dynamics in Nairobi's Informal Settlements,* African Population and Health Research Centre, Nairobi

Baker, J and Mwaiselage, A (1993) *Three Town Study in Tanzania,* Sida, Stockholm

Budds J and McGranahan G. 2003. *Privatization and the provision of Urban Water and Sanitation in Africa,* Asia and Latin America. IIED, London

Cities Alliance (2002) *Shelter Finance for the Poor,* CIVIS, April, November, and others, Shelter for the Poor Series, SEWA Bank, Micasa, and FUNHAVI

Cohen, B (2003) 'Urban Growth in Developing Countries: A Review of Current Trends and a Caution Regarding Existing Forecasts', *World Development, Elsevier,* vol 32 no 1, pages 23-51, January

COHRE (2002) *Global survey 8, Forced Evictions, Violation of Human Rights,* Centre on Housing Rights and Evictions, Geneva

D'Cruz Celine and Satterthwaite, David (2005) *Building Homes, Changing the Official Approaches: The Work of Urban Poor Organizations and their Federations and their Contributions to Meeting the Millennium Development Goals in Urban Areas,* IIED, London

Davis, J (2004) 'Corruption in public water supply; Experiences from South Asia's water and sanitation sector', *World Development, Elsevier,* vol 32 no 1

de Soto, Hernando (1989) *The Other Path: The invisible revolution in the Third World,* I B Taurus, London

Deshingkar, Priya and Anderson, Edward (2004) *People on the move: New policy challenges for increasingly mobile populations,* ODI Natural Resource Perspectives no 92, Overseas Development Institute, London

Dowall, David (1999) 'Globalization, Structural Change and Urban Land Management', *Land Lines,* vol 11 no 1

Driskell, David (2002) *Creating Better Cities with Children and Youth: A Manual for Participation* / David Driskell in collaboration with members of the Growing Up in Cities Project. London : Earthscan ; Paris : UNESCO, 2002.

Dyson, Tim (2003) 'HIV/AIDS and urbanization', *Population and Development Review,* vol 29 no 3, Sept 03: 427-442

Environment & Urbanization vol 14 no 1 and vol 15 no 2, IIED, London

Estache, Antonio, Gomez-Lobo, Andres and Leipziger Danny (2000) *Utilities 'Privatization' and the Poor's Needs in Latin America: Have We Learned Enough to Get It Right?* Paper presented at Conference on Infrastructure for Development: Private Solutions and the Poor, 31 May – 2 June 2000, London

Fay, Marianne, ed. (2005) *The Urban Poor in Latin America*, The World Bank.

Flodman Becker, Kristina (2004) *The Informal Economy: Fact finding study*, Sida, Stockholm

Freire, Mila and Polèse, Mario (2003) *Connecting Cities with Macro-economic Concerns: The Missing Link*, World Bank, Washington, DC

Guasch, J. Luis and Joseph Kogan. 2003. *Just-in-Case Inventories: A Cross-Country Analysis*, Policy Research Working Paper 3012, World Bank, Washington DC.

Hardoy, Jorge E & Satterthwaite, David (1989) *Squatter Citizen: Life in the Urban Third World*, Earthscan, London

Harris, Clive, Hodges, John, Schur, Michael and Shukla, Padmesh (2003) 'Infrastructure Projects—A Review of Cancelled Private Projects', Note 252 in the series *Public Policy for the Private Sector*, World Bank, Washington, DC

Hook, Walter and Howe, John (2004) *Transport and the Millennium Development Goals*, Background report for UN Millennium Project, Institute for Transportation and Development Policy, New York, International Institute for Infrastructural, Hydraulic and Environmental Engineering, Delft, Netherlands

IIED Human Settlements Programme (2006) *A pro-poor urban agenda for Africa: Clarifying ecological and development issues for poor and vulnerable populations.* Human Settlements Discussion Paper Series: Urban Change-2, March 2006.

ILO (2002) *Women and men in the informal economy – A statistical picture*, International Labour Organization, Geneva

International Union of Tenants (2005) *Global Tenant*, Aug 2005, IUT, Stockholm

Kerf, Michel, Gray, R David, Irwin, Timothy, Levesque, Céline and Taylor, Robert R (1998) *Concessions for Infrastructure: A Guide to their Design and Award*, World Paper no 399 Finance, Private Sector, and Infrastructure Network, World Bank, Washington, DC

Kessides, Ioannis N (2004) *Reforming Infrastructure – Privatization, Regulation, and Competition*, World Bank, Washington, DC and Oxford University Press, Oxford

Kikeri, Sunita and Nellis John (2004) 'An Assessment of Privatization', *The World Bank Research Observer*, vol 19 no 1, WB, Washington, DC

Le Blanc, David (2005) *Economic Evaluation of Housing Subsidy Systems: A Methodology with Application to Morocco*, Policy Research Working Paper 3529, World Bank, Washington, DC

Lee, Kyu Sik, Alex Anas and Gi-Taik Oh (1996) *Costs of Infrastructure – Deficiencies in Manufacturing in Indonesia, Nigeria, and Thailand.* Policy Research Working Paper 1604. Washington, DC: The World Bank

Mayo, Stephen K (1999) *Subsidies in Housing,* Sustainable Development Department Technical Papers Series, Inter-American Development Bank, Washington, DC

McGranahan G and Songsore J (1994) 'Wealth, health, and the urban household: Weighing environmental burdens in Accra, Jakarta and São Paulo', *Environment* 36(6) p 40-45

McGranahan, Gordon and Satterthwaite, David (2004) *Governance and Getting the Private Sector to Provide Better Water and Sanitation Services to the Urban Poor,* IIED, London

Milbert Isabelle. 1999. *What Future for Urban Cooperation? Assessment of post Habitat II strategies.* Swiss Agency for Development and Cooperation (SDC), Bern

Mitlin, Diana and Satterthwaite, David (2004) *Empowering Squatter Citizen: Local Government, Civil Society and Urban Poverty Reduction,* Earthscan, London

Mitlin, Diana (2004) *Understanding urban poverty; what the poverty Reduction Strategy Papers tell us,* Poverty Reduction in Urban Areas Series, Working Paper 13, IIED, London

Montgomery, Mark R, Stren, Richard, Cohen, Barney and Reed, Holly E (2004) *Cities Transformed: Demographic Change and its Implications in the Developing World,* For the Panel on Population Dynamics, National Research Council, Earthscan, London

Moser, Caroline (2004) Editorial: 'Urban violence and insecurity: an introductory roadmap', *Environment & Urbanization* (2004) vol 16 no 2, October 2004, IIED, London

National Bureau of Statistics of Tanzania, *Household Survey 2000/2001,* NBS, Dar es Salaam

Nordin, Benita and Östberg, Tommy (2000) *Urban Growth and Cadastral Development – a manual for the development of appropriate cadastral methods for cities and towns in developing countries,* Swedesurvey and Sida, Gävle and Stockholm

Panaritis, Elena (2001) 'Do Property Rights Matter? An Urban Case Study from

Peru', *Global Outlook: International Urban Research Monitor 1* (April): 20–22, Woodrow Wilson International Center for Scholars and US Department of Housing and Urban Development, Washington, DC

Payne, Geoffrey (1998) *Research on public/private partnerships in urban land development*, Paper presented at the 15th Inter-School Conference on Development: 'The Management of Sustainable Development in Fast Growing Urban Areas', University of Wales, Cardiff

Payne, Geoffrey (2003) *Regulatory Guidelines for Affordable Shelter*, Paper Presented at International Workshop on Regulatory Guidelines for Urban Upgrading (RGUU), arranged by ITDG International workshop – March 2003

Red Cross/Red Crescent (1998) *World disaster report 1998*, Oxford University Press, Oxford

Reinikka, Ritva and Svensson, Jakob (1999) *Confronting Competition: Investment Response and Constraints in Uganda.* Policy Research Working Paper 2242. World Bank, Washington, DC

Satterthwaite, David (2005) *The scale of urban change world-wide 1950-2000 and its underpinning*, IIED, London (http://www.iied.org/urban/index.html)

Satterthwaite, David (2004) *The under-estimation of urban poverty in low and middle-income nation*, Poverty Reduction in Urban Areas Series, Working Paper 14, IIED, London

Schneider, Wolf (1960) *Überall ist Babylon*, Econ-Verlag, Düsseldorf

Shah, Anwar and Thompson, Theresa (2002) *Implementing Decentralized Local Governance: A Treacherous Road with Potholes, Detours and Road Closures*, Paper presented at the conference 'Can Decentralization Help Rebuild Indonesia?' sponsored by the Andrew Young School of Policy Studies, Georgia State University, Atlanta, Georgia, May 1-3, 2002

Sida (1999) *Urban transport in Swedish development cooperation*, Stockholm

Sida (2002) *Perspectives on Poverty*, Stockholm

Sida (2004) *A Future for the Past; Historic Cities in Development*, Stockholm

Sida (2005) *Urban Assets; Cultural Heritage as a Tool for Development*, Stockholm

Sida (2005) *Caring for the Historic Environment*, Stockholm

Singh, B N (1983) *Research Model for Urban Land and Infrastructure Pricing, Costing and Design: A Case Study of Uttar Pradesh, India*, World Bank, Transport and Urban Development Department, Washington, DC

Smolka, Martim (2002) *Secure Tenure for the Urban Poor*, Presentation to the Cities Alliance on May 23, 2002, The Cities Alliance, Washington, DC

Tannerfeldt, Göran (1995) *Towards an Urban World*, Sida, Stockholm

UN (1996) *The Habitat Agenda*
  (www.unhabitat.org/declarations/habitat_agenda.asp), UN, New York

UNCHS (2001) *Cities in a Globalizing World: Global Report on Human Settlements*,
  Earthscan, London

UNDP (1996) *Urban Agriculture: Food, Jobs and Sustainable Cities*, United Nations
  Development Programme, New York

UN Department of Economic and Social Affairs, Population Division (2004)
  World Population Prospects: The 2003 Revision, UN, New York
  (www.unpopulation.org)

UN Department of Economic and Social Affairs, Population Division (2004)
  World Urbanization Prospects – 2003 Revision, UN, New York

UN-HABITAT (2004) *The State of the World's Cities 2004/2005: Globalization and
  urban culture*, Earthscan, London

UN-HABITAT (2003) *The Challenge of Slums: Global Report on Human Settlements 2003*, Earthscan, London

UN-HABITAT (2003) *Water and Sanitation in the World's Cities: Local action for
  global goals*, Earthscan, London

UN-HABITAT (2005) *Financing Urban Shelter: Global Report on Human Settlements 2005*, Earthscan, London

UN Millennium Project, Task Force on Water and Sanitation (2005) *Health, Dignity and Development: What Will it Take?* Earthscan, London

UN Millennium Project, Task Force on Improving the Lives of Slum Dwellers,
  (2005) *A home in the city*, Earthscan, London

Walker, Ian, Ordonez, Fidel, Serrano, Pedro and Halpern, Jonathan (2004) *Pri-
  cing, Subsidies and the Poor: Demand for Improved Water Services in Central
  America*, Policy Research Working Paper 2468, World Bank, Washington,
  DC

Winblad, Uno and Simpson-Hébert, Mayling (2004) *Ecological Sanitation*, Stockholm Environment Institute, Stockholm

World Bank (1993) *Housing: Enabling Markets to Work*, WB, Washington DC

World Bank (1994) *World Development Report 1994: Infrastructure for
  Development*, Oxford University Press, New York

World Bank (2004) *World Development Indicators 2004*, WB, Washington DC

World Bank (2005) *Private Participation in Infrastructure Database*. (Can be found
  at http://ppi.worldbank.org/), WB, Washington DC

World Panel on Financing Water Infrastructure (2003) *Financing Water for All*,
  The World Water Council and the Global Water Partnership, Marseille

About the authors

Göran Tannerfeldt, architect SAR/MSA, is a senior advisor on urban development with more than forty years of international experience. He has initiated and developed the urban program of the Swedish International Development Cooperation Agency (Sida) and was head of its Urban Division. He is the author of *Towards an Urban World* (Sida, 1995).

Per Ljung, PhD, is Chairman and CEO of PM Global Infrastructure, a firm that specializes in infrastructure reform and financing. He has headed the World Bank's operational division dealing with urban development in North Africa and the Middle East as well as been chief of its central unit for policy development and research in the urban development field. Recently, his focus has been on innovative financing mechanisms for municipal infrastructure, low-income housing and slum upgrading.